Contents

D1391854

www.shoot.co.uk

Pedigree Published by Pedigree Books Ltd.

PEDIGREE BOOKS, BEECH HILL HOUSE, WALNUT GARDENS,
EXETER, DEVON EX4 4DH
shoot@pedigreegroup.co.uk

EDITOR COLIN MITCHELL **DESIGN** RICHARD GRACE

£7.99

WE ARE THE CHAMPIONS... AGAIN!

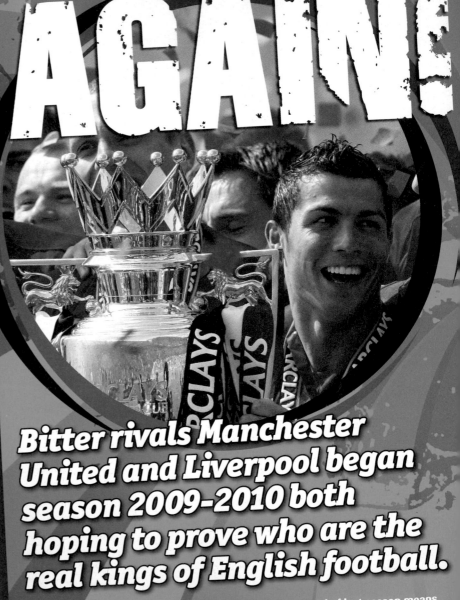

Premier League appearances by United's 2008-09 heroes

Nemanja Vidic	34
Cristiano Ronaldo	33
Edwin van der Sar	33
Dimitar Berbatov	32
John O'Shea	30
Wayne Rooney	30
Carlos Tevez	29
Michael Carrick	28
Patrice Evra	28
Ryan Giggs	28
Darren Fletcher	26
Ji-Sung Park	25
Rio Ferdinand	24
Paul Scholes	21
Anderson	17
Jonny Evans	17
Gary Neville	15
Rafael Da Silva	15
Nani	12
Wes Brown	7
Tomasz Kuszczak	3
Federico Macheda	3
Ben Foster	2
Darren Gibson	2
Owen Hargreaves	2
Danny Welbeck	2
Richard Eckersley	1
Zoran Tosic	1

Bitter rivals Manchester United and Liverpool began season 2009-2010 both hoping to prove who are the real kings of English football.

UNITED'S THIRD Premier League victory in a row at the end of last season means that they have now won 18 top-flight titles - the same number as Liverpool.

Although the Anfield aces have yet to win a Premier League title, they have also won 18 English league titles over the years.

But they know they now have a very long way to go to rival the 11 titles United have captured since the Premier League began in season 1992-93.

Wicked winger Cristiano Ronaldo once again made a major difference to United. Despite a slow start to the season the Portugal star finished up as the club's top Premier League scorer with 18 goals (26 in all games) - six ahead of England striker Wayne Rooney.

Hard man defender Nemanja Vidic, who picked up his third title and weighed in with four vital goals, was named the club's Player of the Season.

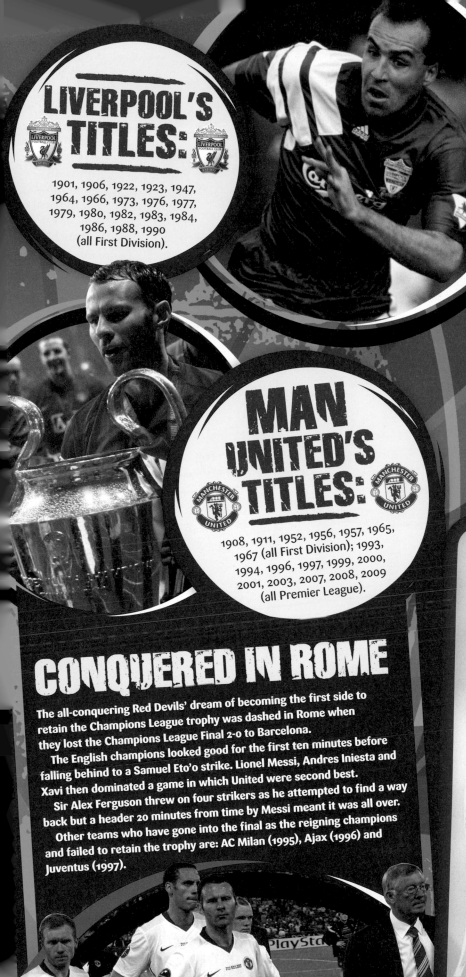

LIVERPOOL'S TITLES:

1901, 1906, 1922, 1923, 1947, 1964, 1966, 1973, 1976, 1977, 1979, 1980, 1982, 1983, 1984, 1986, 1988, 1990 (all First Division).

MAN UNITED'S TITLES:

1908, 1911, 1952, 1956, 1957, 1965, 1967 (all First Division); 1993, 1994, 1996, 1997, 1999, 2000, 2001, 2003, 2007, 2008, 2009 (all Premier League).

UNITED THE BEST? NOT QUITE...

Man United, Liverpool and Barcelona all have one thing in common – 18 top-flight domestic titles to their name.

But all three giant clubs trail behind 11 other teams when it comes to the overall list of titles won by major European clubs.

Rangers head the table with a staggering 52 league titles to their name, closely followed by Glasgow rivals Celtic on 42.

Also ahead of the two English clubs are: Olympiakos (Greece) 37, Real Madrid (Spain) 31, Benfica (Portugal) 31, Ajax (Holland) 29, Juventus (Italy) 27, Porto (Portugal) 24, PSV Eindhoven (Holland) 21, Bayern Munich (Germany) 21, Panathinaikos (Greece) 19.

CONQUERED IN ROME

The all-conquering Red Devils' dream of becoming the first side to retain the Champions League trophy was dashed in Rome when they lost the Champions League Final 2-0 to Barcelona.

The English champions looked good for the first ten minutes before falling behind to a Samuel Eto'o strike. Lionel Messi, Andres Iniesta and Xavi then dominated a game in which United were second best.

Sir Alex Ferguson threw on four strikers as he attempted to find a way back but a header 20 minutes from time by Messi meant it was all over.

Other teams who have gone into the final as the reigning champions and failed to retain the trophy are: AC Milan (1995), Ajax (1996) and Juventus (1997).

Final Premier League table 2008-09

1	Man United	38	44	90
2	Liverpool	38	50	86
3	Chelsea	38	44	83
4	Arsenal	38	31	72
5	Everton	38	18	63
6	Aston Villa	38	6	62
7	Fulham	38	5	53
8	Tottenham	38	0	51
9	West Ham	38	-3	51
10	Man City	38	8	50
11	Wigan	38	-11	45
12	Stoke	38	-17	45
13	Bolton	38	-12	41
14	Portsmouth	38	-19	41
15	Blackburn	38	-20	41
16	Sunderland	38	-20	36
17	Hull	38	-25	35
18	Newcastle	38	-19	34
19	Middlesbrough	38	-29	32
20	West Brom	38	-31	32

Cup of cheer
"Lots of people tend to regard the Premier League and Champions League as the only trophies that matter but for me the FA Cup is magical. I remember going to Wembley when I was nine to see Everton beat United 1-0 and can remember every single minute."

Losing hurts
"I was man of the match when we lost the [FA Cup Final] to Arsenal on penalties and the award meant absolutely nothing to me. I've still got the trophy and it's a little reminder of how much it hurts when you lose."

WAYNE'S A WINNER!

ENGLAND AND MAN UNITED striker Wayne Rooney on how much it means to him to win silverware

Friendly fire
"Friendly games are different to qualifiers but we always have a point to prove. We believe we have the players to do well in major tournaments. We haven't done so in recent years but hopefully this can change for us."

Simply the best
"Before every big tournament fans expect a lot of big things from players and the players want to give them something to be happy about. No matter what the performances though the players always give their best."

Duty to win

"When you become a Manchester United player you take on responsibility to try and win every trophy you compete for. The feeling of success doesn't last long at this club. You have the celebration and that's it!"

Price of success

"Success makes you hungrier for more trophies. When you win a trophy you know it will be even more disappointing if you don't win it again the next season. If you don't retain that trophy it can't be regarded as anything but a failure."

If the cap fits...

"I want to win more trophies, earn more caps and score more goals. It is every player's aim to win a trophy with England. If we could do that in the next few years I'm sure everyone - from the fans, the players and the staff involved - would be absolutely delighted."

Being a Lion...

"I still get shivers down my spine when I step out onto the pitch for England."

Did you know?

Man United fans refer to Rooney as **'EL BLANCO PELE'** – which translates as 'The White Pele!'

Wayne has a blue Celtic cross tattoo on his right arm with the word **"COLEEN"** above it.

Wazza became England's **YOUNGEST-EVER GOALSCORER**, when aged just 17, he scored in the 53rd minute of England's 2-1 victory over Macedonia in 2003.

He grew up as a massive **EVERTON** fan and was even a club mascot as a 12-year-old.

Compliments of the season

Who won what in 2008-09

CHAMPIONSHIP CHAMPIONS

Wolves

| AUTOMATIC PROMOTION BIRMINGHAM CITY | PLAY-OFF FINAL BURNLEY 1 SHEFFIELD UNITED 0 |

LEAGUE ONE CHAMPIONS

Leicester City

AUTOMATIC PROMOTION PETERBOROUGH	PLAY-OFF FINAL MILLWALL 2 SCUNTHORPE 3

LEAGUE TWO CHAMPIONS

Brentford

AUTOMATIC PROMOTION EXETER CITY AND WYCOMBE	PLAY-OFF FINAL SHREWSBURY 0 GILLINGHAM 1

BLUE SQUARE PREMIER CHAMPIONS

Burton Albion

PLAY-OFF FINAL
CAMBRIDGE 0 TORQUAY 2

SCOTTISH PREMIER LEAGUE

Rangers

Seven points behind massive rivals Celtic at one stage of the season, Gers won the league by four points. It was a world record 52nd title for Rangers who regained the trophy after it had gone to Parkhead following the three previous campaigns.

SCOTTISH CUP

Rangers

Gers completed the League and cup double thanks to a 1-0 victory over Falkirk. Spanish striker Nacho Novo scored the spectacular winner in the 46th minute – just 36 seconds after arriving as a substitute.

★ CIS CUP ★

Celtic

Just 90 seconds into extra-time Darren O'Dea gave Celtic the lead against cup holders Rangers. With seconds remaining Aiden McGeady made it 2-0 from the penalty spot after Gers Kirk Broadfoot had been sent-off for a foul on the midfielder in front of more than 51,000 fans.

★ CARLING CUP ★

Manchester United

Cup holders Spurs kept it goal-less for 120 minutes against Man United but fell at the final hurdle losing 4-1 in the penalty shoot-out. Ryan Giggs scored before keeper Ben Foster saved Jamie O'Hara's effort. Tevez and Ronaldo both scored, Corluka notched for Spurs, but David Bentley shot wide. Anderson's spot-kick sealed the victory.

★ FA CUP ★

Chelsea

Everton's first appearance in the final in 14 years got off to a flyer with the fastest FA Cup Final goal ever, Louis Saha sticking the ball in the net after just 25 seconds. But Didier Drogba's header after 21 minutes brought the scores level and Frank Lampard's long distance goal in the 71st clinched the Blues second FA Cup in three seasons.

JOHNSTONE'S PAINTS TROPHY

Luton Town

The Hatters started the season with a staggering 30-point deduction and could never have imagined winning a 3-2 thriller at Wembley in extra-time. Hooper gave Scunthorpe the lead before Martin and Craddock put Town in front. Grant McCann forced extra time with his 88th minute equaliser but Claude Gnakpa hit the winner for Mick Harford's side in the 95th minute.

The FA Trophy

STEVENAGE BOROUGH
The Hertfordshire outfit won the trophy for the second time in three seasons. They beat Conference rivals York City 2-0 at Wembley with goals from Steve Morison and Lee Boylan.

The FA Vase

WHITLEY BAY
First half goals by Lee Kerr and Paul Chow sealed Bay's Vase victory against first-time finalists Glossop. The north easterners last won the Vase in 2002.

UEFA CUP

SHAKHTAR DONETSK
The final UEFA Cup Final – the competition is now known as the Europa League – was won in Istanbul by Ukrainian side Shakhtar Donetsk who beat Germans Werder Bremen 2-1.

PFA

Ryan Giggs

Amazingly for a player who has won so many awards during such an illustrious career, this was the first time 35-year-old Giggsy had won the PFA award. He was twice PFA Young Player of the Year. The man who has appeared and scored in every Premier League since it began, beat off the challenge of Old Trafford team-mates, Rio Ferdinand, Nemanja Vidic, Cristiano Ronaldo and Edwin van der Sar plus Liverpool's Steven Gerrard.

PFA YOUNG PLAYER OF THE YEAR

Ashley Young

Aston Villa's high-speed winger saw off a challenge from club and England team-mate Gabriel Agbonlahor, Manchester United's Jonny Evans and Rafael Da Silva, Aaron Lennon of Spurs and Manchester City's Stephen Ireland, to lift the trophy.

FOOTBALLER WRITERS' PLAYER OF THE YEAR

Steven Gerrard

Stevie G became the first Liverpool player since John Barnes in 1990 to win this award. He was the only Anfield player on a shortlist that included Chelsea's Frank Lampard plus six Man United stars. Ryan Giggs and Wayne Rooney were second and third.

Euro stars

The teams that conquered Europe's major leagues during season 2008-09

Spain
CHAMPIONS: Barcelona RUNNERS-UP: Real Madrid

Italy
CHAMPIONS: Inter Milan RUNNERS-UP: Juventus

France
CHAMPIONS: Bordeaux RUNNERS-UP: Marseille

Germany
CHAMPIONS: Wolfsburg RUNNERS-UP: B. Munich

Holland
CHAMPIONS: AZ Alkmaar RUNNERS-UP: FC Twente

10 THINGS YOU NEED TO KNOW ABOUT ARSENAL STAR

Andrey Arshavin

1 Andrey Sergeyevich Arshavin was born on May 29, 1981 in Leningrad. He can operate in midfield or as a striker. He made more than 300 appearances in all competitions for Zenit St. Petersburg before his move to Arsenal.

2 The 2006 Russia Player of the Year cost the Gunners around £15m but this could rise by another £2m or so depending on the striker's progress. Arshavin agreed a four-year deal.

3 His transfer during the January 2009 transfer window nearly never happened. The paperwork reached the Football Association in time but it had to be rubber stamped after the deadline once a few minor errors were sorted out.

4 There are reports that the player coughed up £1m of his own money so that he could move to The Emirates Stadium. That's not impossible as players in the Russian Premier League can earn big money.

5 Arshavin hadn't played a match since the previous November and was not fit when he arrived in London. He'd been tracked by a number of top clubs - including Barcelona - since his performances at Euro 2008 that earned him a place in UEFA's Team of the Tournament.

7 Andrey is very fashion conscious. Not only has he designed dresses since he was 17, but he has also flown a hairdresser from Russia to London to sort out his barnet!

6 The player was too shy to go through Arsenal's initiation ceremony where new arrivals at The Emirates Stadium have to sing or make a speech. He was asked to recite his favourite song but wouldn't climb on a restaurant table to perform.

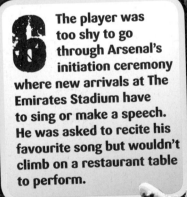

8 He's turned out more than 40 times for Russia since making his international debut in 2002. His first international goal came eight months after his first start, in a friendly against Romania.

9 During his time at Zenit, Arshavin won the Russian Premier League, Russian Cup, Russian Super Cup, UEFA Cup and UEFA Super Cup.

10 There have been wildly conflicting reports about the player's wage demands - with suggestions that he is getting paid £67,000 a week whilst others suggest he wouldn't have moved for less than £80,000. What's a few quid between friends?

Andrey
Arshavin

PUZZLE TIME!

Get shirty

YOU ARE SMART enough to know where the top-class players pictured below play now – but do you recognise them playing for their previous teams? Warning – one of the players has NOT played in the shirt that our clever designer has pictured him in. We want to know the players, the team... plus the odd one out!

1 Player
Team

2 Player
Team

3 Player
Team

4 Player
Team

5 Player
Team

6 Player
Team

True or false?

A MICHAEL OWEN WAS A GOOD BOXER WHEN HE WAS YOUNG.

TRUE ◯
FALSE ◯

B WAYNE ROONEY IS A BIG FAN OF OASIS.

TRUE ◯ FALSE ◯

C JAMES BEATTIE WAS ONCE A CHAMPION SWIMMER.

TRUE ◯
FALSE ◯

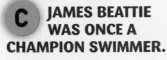

D HARRY REDKNAPP LOVES RACING HIS DOGS.

TRUE ◯
FALSE ◯

E JIMMY BULLARD IS A HIGHLY RATED MATCH ANGLER.

TRUE ◯
FALSE ◯

F PETER CROUCH WAS AN ACE HURDLER.

TRUE ◯
FALSE ◯

G JERMAIN DEFOE IS A DEVOUT CHRISTIAN.

TRUE ◯
FALSE ◯

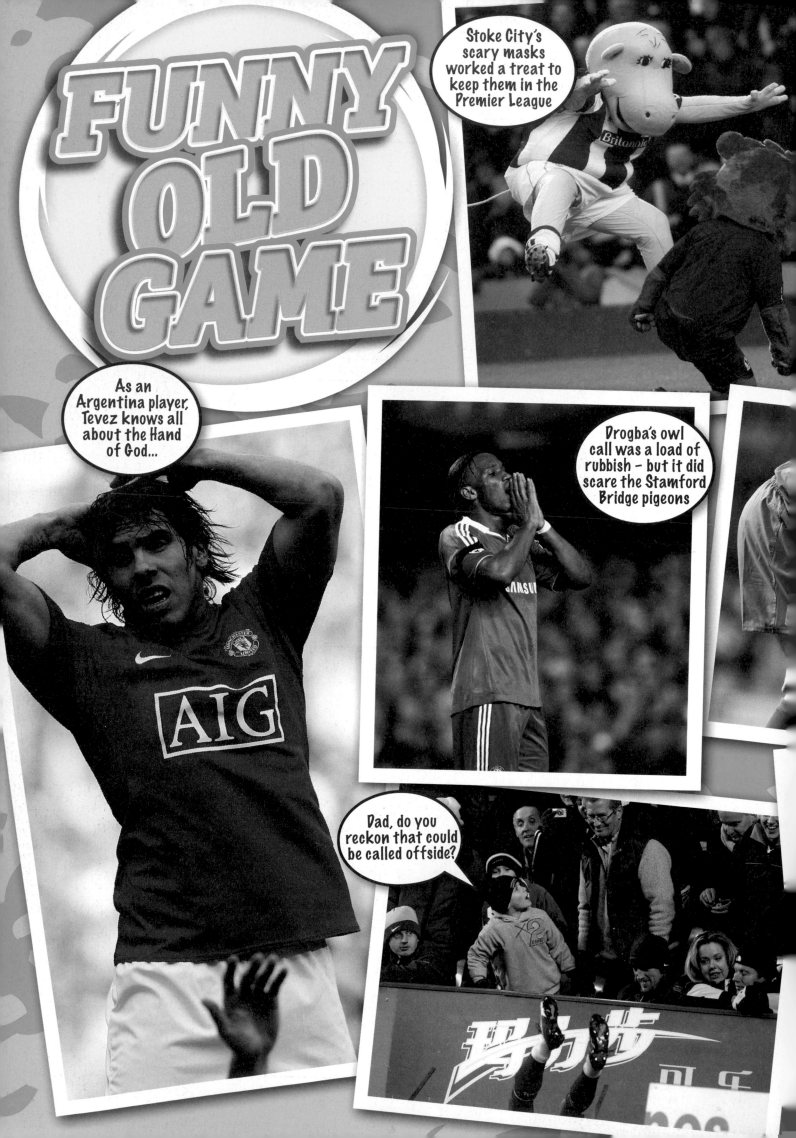

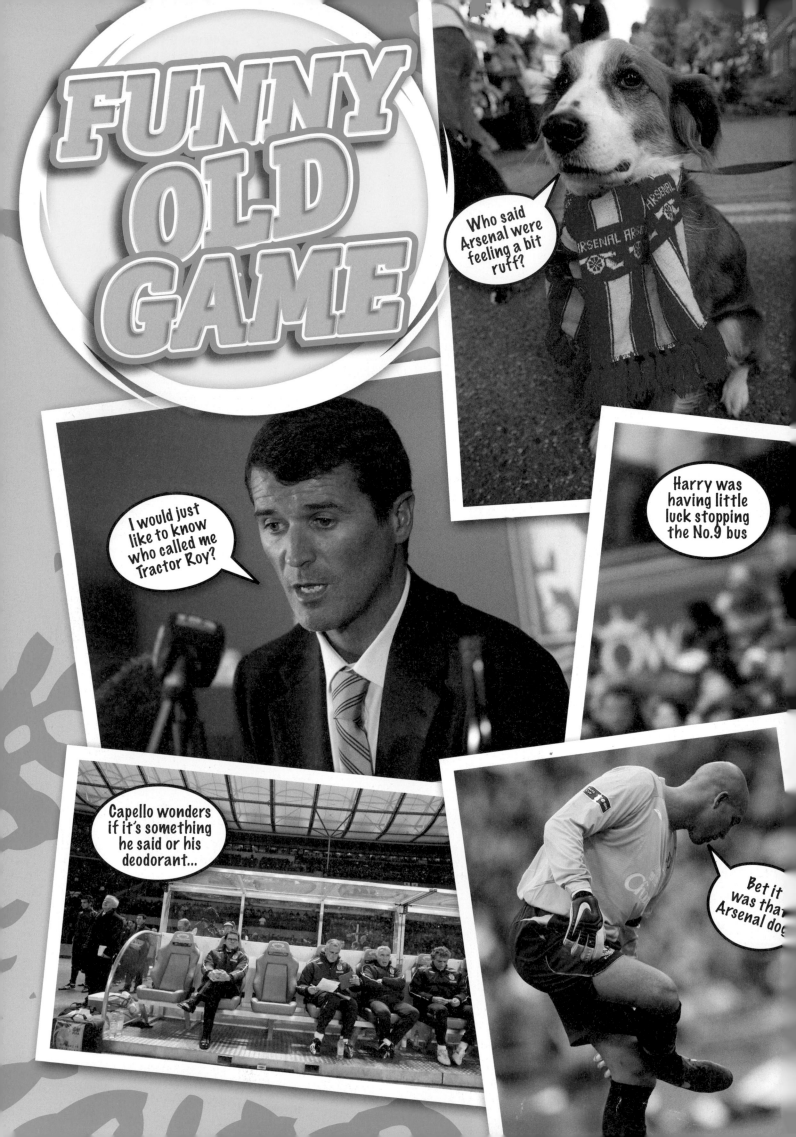

Ones to watch

BEN AMOS

Date of birth:
April 10, 1990
Place of birth:
Macclesfield
Position: Keeper
International:
England

The teenager has been with Manchester United since the age of 11 and made his first-team debut in the Carling Cup last term. Has appeared at Under-18, 19 and 20 level for England.

ADAM LALLANA

Date of birth:
May 10, 1988
Place of birth: St. Albans, Hertfordshire
Position: Midfielder
International: England

Tottenham and Fulham both tried to prize the promising midfielder away from Southampton. Saints admitted they would have to part with the player at the right price. An attacking midfielder, Adam came through the Saints youth ranks and has played for England Under-18 and 21s.

LEWIS McGUGAN

Date of birth:
October 25, 1988
Place of birth:
Nottingham
Position: Midfielder
International: England

McGugan came through England's Under-16, 17 and 18 ranks with the likes of Theo Walcott and Lee Cattermole and is rated as one of the best players outside of the Premier League. Injuries held back his career at Nottingham Forest but he has bags of fight, ability and the knack of scoring some great goals.

JAMES TOMKINS

Date of birth:
March 29, 1989
Place of birth:
Basildon, Essex
Position: Defender
International:
England

Yet another young star to roll of the West Ham production line, Tomkins has played at every England level from Under-15 to Under-21. Loaned to Derby early in season 2008-09, he returned and made 14 first-team appearances for the Hammers.

CHRIS SMALLING

Date of birth:
November 22, 1989
Place of birth:
Greenwich, London
Position: Central-defender
International: England

Fulham snapped up the player from non-league Maidstone United and handed him a three-year deal in summer 2008. He quickly made the jump from Isthmian Premier League to Premier League reserves and soon earned a place in the Cottagers' first-team squad. Has played for England at schoolboy and Under-20 level.

JUNIOR STANISLAS

Date of birth:
November 26, 1989
Place of birth:
Kidbrooke, South London
Position: Midfielder
International: England

The West Ham Academy graduate has played for his country at various junior levels. Had a spell on loan at Southend United but is now contracted to Upton Park until 2013.

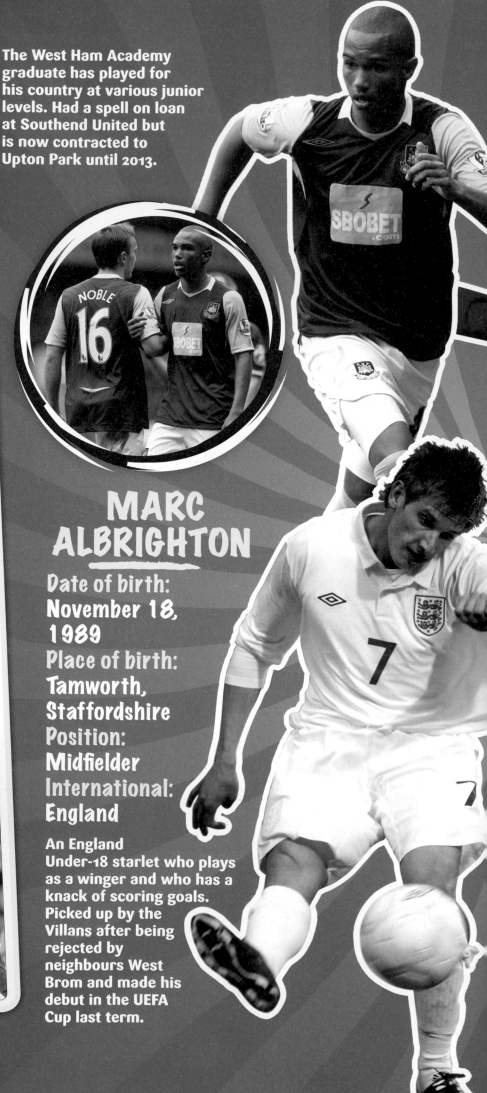

KEVIN McDONALD

Date of birth:
November 4, 1988
Place of birth:
Carnoustie
Position: Midfielder
International:
Scotland

A Scotland Under-19 and 21 player, the former Dundee star cost Burnley around £500,000. Now he has the chance to prove himself in the Premier League.

MARC ALBRIGHTON

Date of birth:
November 18, 1989
Place of birth:
Tamworth, Staffordshire
Position:
Midfielder
International:
England

An England Under-18 starlet who plays as a winger and who has a knack of scoring goals. Picked up by the Villans after being rejected by neighbours West Brom and made his debut in the UEFA Cup last term.

DANNY DRINKWATER

Date of birth: March 5, 1990
Place of birth: Manchester
Position: Midfielder
International: England

Injury has prevented Danny making the big breakthrough everyone at United expects. He's been with the club since the age of nine and can use both feet to pick out great passes. He is believed to be the player who lives nearest to Old Trafford!

JOSH WALKER

Date of birth:
February 21, 1989
Place of birth:
Newcastle-upon-Tyne
Position: Midfielder
International: England

A Three Lions captain at Under-16, 17 and 18 levels, Josh has had loan spells at Bournemouth and Aberdeen. A knee injury held back his development but Boro gave him a deal to 2011.

10 THINGS YOU NEED TO KNOW ABOUT MAN UNITED STAR

Nemanja Vidic

1 Nemanja Vidic was born in Titovo Uzice, Yugoslavia on October 21, 1981. He is 6ft 2in tall and is married to Ana with a young son called Luka.

2 The hard-man central-defender played for Red Star Belgrade, Spartak Subotica (loan) and Spartak Moscow before joining Manchester United in 2006. He cost United £7m and was at first written off as a poor buy by Old Trafford supporters - now he has cult status!

3 He played for Yugoslavia but after civil war in his country he became part of the Serbia and Montenegro side and is now in the Serbia team. A training ground injury prevented him appearing for Serbia during the 2006 World Cup finals. He appeared for Yugoslavia at Euro 2004.

4 The Serbian is known by his team-mates as 'Vida'. His partnership with Rio Ferdinand has been described by Sir Alex Ferguson as the club's best since Gary Pallister and Steve Bruce in the early 1990s.

5 When he arrived in England he couldn't speak the language, other than words he had picked up from watching movies. He admits his first three months were very difficult - especially trying to understand the accents of quiet guy Paul Scholes and Scotsman Darren Fletcher!

6 Vidic made his Manchester United debut in the Carling Cup semi-final victory over Blackburn in 2006, 20 days after signing. He collected a winner's medal after appearing in the final as a sub.

7 Many fans believed Vidic was Man of the Match as Man United won the Champions League Final against Chelsea - although the award went to United keeper Edwin van der Sar who saved a vital penalty.

8 Vidic won his first Premier League Player of the Month award in January 2009 as United went through that period without conceding a goal and set a new record of 11 clean sheets. He also scored goals against Chelsea and West Brom.

9 United's biggest rivals, Liverpool, started transfer talks with Vidic who was also chased by Italians Fiorentina - but the player reckons he made the right choice in moving to Old Trafford.

10 Money isn't everything - and Vidic admits that Spartak offered him more cash than Man United if he would stay in Russia. But he wanted to see if he could make the grade in the Premier League and has agreed a deal to 2012.

Nemanja Vidic

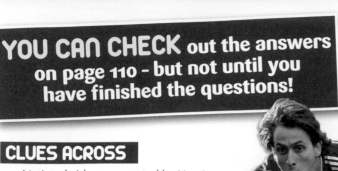

GIANT

YOU CAN CHECK out the answers on page 110 – but not until you have finished the questions!

CLUES ACROSS

1 National side represented by Yossi Benayoun and Tal Ben Haim (6)
4 Homeland of Gallas, Silvestre and Clichy (6)
8 - - - Diaby, Paris-born midfielder who joined Arsenal from Auxerre (4)
9 Striker, - - - Zamora, whose London clubs include Tottenham, West Ham and Fulham (5)
10 Craven Cottage's Hungary captain, Zoltan (4)
13 Dave, Stoke's 6ft 3in striker loaned back to Reading last season (6)
14 Premier League club, Blackburn - - - (6)
16 Real Madrid's Brazil striker sold to Manchester City in 2008 (7)
18 28 year-old Ireland midfield man who moved from MK Dons to Ewood Park last year (7)
19 - - - Campbell, former England centre-back of Spurs, Arsenal and Portsmouth fame (3)
20 The Canaries, Norfolk club relegated from the Championship in 2009 (7)
22 Liverpool and Spain right-back, Alvaro (7)
25 French-born Cameroon left-back, Benoit Assou - - -, in England with Spurs (6)
27 Sean - - - Phillips, Manchester City and England winger (6)
30 Barcelona and Cameroon goal machine, Samuel (4)
31 What players do every day of the week to ensure they stay fit for games (5)
32 Darren, England striker who's scored for Ipswich, Charlton and Spurs (4)
33 Nicky, veteran Hull midfielder who's been with Leeds, Liverpool and Everton (6)
34 Arsenal's French manager, - - - Wenger (6)

CLUES DOWN

2 and 6 Down England midfielder of Charlton, Chelsea, Newcastle and West Ham (5,6)
3 Club emblem of Millwall FC (4)
4 - - - Aurelio, Liverpool left full-back from Brazil (5)
5 Stoke City's former Leeds United forward, Richard (9)
6 See 2 Down
7 Bustling Bolton front man, Kevin, who joined Bolton from Saints in 2006 (6)
11 and 26 Down Chelsea stalwart who captains England (4,5)
12 Steven, Blackburn's Republic of Ireland international whose season was ruined by injury (4)
15 Nickname of new Championship side, Peterborough United (4)
17 Manchester United's Champions League Final opponents from Spain (9)
18 - - - Shearer, TV pundit who took over as Newcastle boss in 2009 (4)
20 New Zealand central defender, Ryan, who came to England with Blackburn (6)
21 Scunthorpe United's club nickname (4)
23 Gigg Lane club that reached the Division Two play-offs last season (4)
24 Mikel, Everton's Spanish star whose season was curtailed by injury (6)
26 See 11 Down
28 West Ham United and England keeper, Robert (5)
29 The governing body of world football (1.1.1.1.)

CROSSWORD

Who do you rate?

THAT'S THE QUESTION
we put to some top-class stars to discover the players the professionals admire!

CESC FABREGAS
Arsenal and Spain

NOMINATED BY: MANUEL ALMUNIA, ARSENAL

"The more I see of Cesc the less he surprises me. Everyone in England knows how good he is. We have some fantastic midfielders in Spain but I don't think there are any better than Cesc."

JOHN TERRY
Chelsea and England

NOMINATED BY: JAMIE CARRAGHER, LIVERPOOL

"For me, John Terry is the best centre-back in the world. Over the past few years, I wouldn't have anyone ahead of him."

DAVID BECKHAM
England

NOMINATED BY: KAKA, BRAZIL

"He is a great player with talent and professionalism who can still play in the English, Italian or Spanish championships. He is still a big player and can be at the top level for a long time to come."

AARON RAMSEY
Arsenal and Wales

NOMINATED BY: CRAIG BELLAMY, MAN CITY

"I cannot recall as much fuss about a young Wales player maybe since Ryan Giggs. He is a special talent, we don't get many like him coming through. He has been outstanding whenever I have seen him train or play."

KAKA
Brazil

NOMINATED BY: ROBINHO, MAN CITY

"He is one of the best players in the world. Kaka would be a huge triumph at any club. He is world-class and his technique is unique. He is very professional."

STEVEN GERRARD
Liverpool and England

NOMINATED BY: DANNY GUTHRIE, NEWCASTLE

"Steven Gerrard is the top man, Liverpool's best player. I learned a lot from him. I think he could be the best, especially as he scores goals as well. For a midfielder to score as many as he does is incredible."

Premier League Secrets

Changing sides

PHIL NEVILLE is making plans for when he finally hangs up his boots - and hopes to go into management.

The England midfielder and defender has certainly been in a great position to pick up some good tips having worked at Manchester United with Sir Alex Ferguson and now at Everton with David Moyes.

Phil, younger brother of United's Gary - who is expected to get a coaching role at Old Trafford - is already taking his coaching badges so he is ready for when his playing career ends.

"It's something that interests me but hopefully it's a long way off just yet," said Phil.

Home rules

CRISTIANO RONALDO is becoming a hot-shot in the property world.

In addition to his flash pad in England, the Real Madrid winger has bought four overseas homes and was making moves for a hotel on his home island of Madeira.

The World Player of the Year already has a flat in Portugal but is also having a mega-luxury house built there that includes a swimming pool that is both indoors and outside!

Hot wheels

NIGEL DE JONG is the king of the road at Manchester City!

The Holland midfielder has a hot business souping up flash motors likes Ferraris, Mercedes and Aston Martins.

The £18m star has outlets in Germany and the Middle East and has already interested Dutch colleagues Robin van Persie and Ryan Babel in getting their own hot wheels.

Simply the Becks

DAVID BECKHAM is one of the best-known sportsmen ever to walk the planet but he's got his own football heroes that he's always worshipped.

Becks equalled Bobby Moore's 108-cap England record in 2009 but admits that the former West Ham star is one of his own legends – along with ex-Manchester United star Bobby Charlton.

In fact, Becks was so star-struck as a youngster that he used to collect sticker books and anything else to do with football that he could get his hands on.

He would learn all of the facts and figures on football player cards and could tell you how many caps they had won and games they'd played.

Super shinnies!

EMMANUEL ADEBAYOR won't go anywhere without his super shinpads – even though they are years old!

The superstitious Togo striker was given the adidas pads when he was still a teenager in Africa and he scored for his international team.

"I lost them years ago but then found them again and I use them every day in training and for matches. I believe in these things as I am very superstitious," he admitted.

Did you know?

MAROUANE FELLAINI, Everton's record signing, is nicknamed Screech after the character on Kids TV show Saved by the Bell.

Man United and England defender **RIO FERDINAND** is a big fan of TV programme Gavin and Stacey. Although he gets paid thousands of pounds every week he reportedly phoned the programme's production company and asked for a box set of the whole series!

Liverpool stars **STEVE GERRARD** and **FERNANDO TORRES** have backed a campaign that advertises the club's own brand of aftershave called L4Men, and which carries the team's Liver Bird logo.

SPOT THE BALL

WE'VE MADE THE ball disappear from these pictures of games involving some top teams. Can you mark which of the squares it was in? Answers page 110

1. ARSENAL v HULL CITY
GREAT GUNNERS GRABBED A 2-1 FA CUP VICTORY TO EASE INTO THE SEMI-FINALS

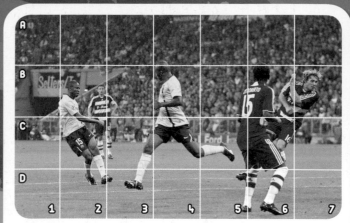

2. BAYERN MUNICH v BARCELONA
SPANISH GIANTS MARCHED ON IN THE CHAMPIONS LEAGUE AFTER A 1-1 DRAW

3. BIRMINGHAM CITY v WOLVES
WOLVES GOT THE BLUES AS THEY CRASHED 2-0 AT THE ST. ANDREWS HOME OF THEIR BIG RIVALS

4. CHELSEA v BOLTON
THE BLUES SAW RED AS THE TROTTERS DRAMATICALLY CLAWED BACK TO 4-3 FROM A 4-0 DEFICIT

5. CHELSEA V LIVERPOOL
STAMFORD BRIDGE WAS STUNNED AS MAJOR RIVALS DRAEW 4-4 IN THE CHAMPIONS LEAGUE

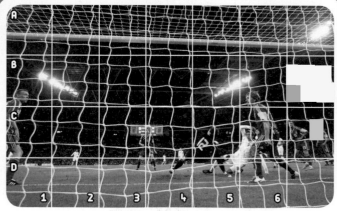

6. ENGLAND v UKRAINE
JOHN TERRY'S LATE WINNER HELPED THE THREE LIONS TO A 2-1 WIN AFTER PETER CROUCH'S OPENER

7. EVERTON v WIGAN

TWO FOR BRAZILIAN JO AS TOFFEES STUCK FOUR PAST ATHLETIC WITHOUT REPLY

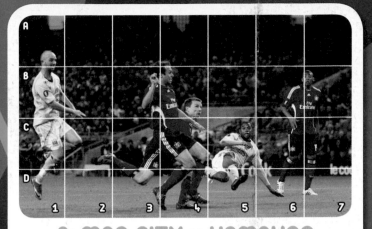

8. MAN CITY v HAMBURG

CITY WON 2-1 BUT MISSED OUT ON THE UEFA CUP SEMI-FINALS IN 4-3 AGGREGATE LOSS

9. MAN UNITED v ASTON VILLA

VILLA'S TWO-GOAL ADVANTAGE DISAPPEARED IN A 3-2 DEFEAT THANKS TO SUPERSUB FEDERICO MACHEDA

10. MAN CITY v FULHAM

DEMPSEY DOUBLE HELPED VISITORS TO 3-1 WIN AS RECORD BUY ROBINHO STAYED ON THE BENCH

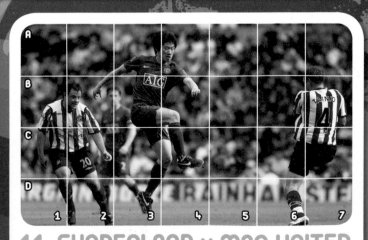

11. SUNDERLAND v MAN UNITED

JUST ONE GOAL FOR THE RED DEVILS IN A TIGHT VICTORY AT THE STADIUM OF LIGHT

10
THINGS YOU NEED TO KNOW ABOUT INTER MILAN STAR

Zlatan Ibrahimovich

1 Zlatan Ibramhimovic was born in Malmo, Sweden – his unusual name is because he has a Bosnian father and Croatian mother, although he was brought up in Sweden.

2 Although he had a choice of international sides he could have turned out for, Zlatan picked Sweden Under-21s and after just seven games graduated to the senior side in 2001. He now has more than 50 caps.

3 The winger-striker began his professional career with his home town club but after two seasons moved to Dutch giants Ajax in 2001 for around £6m.

4 He picked up Dutch League titles in 2002 and 2004 but on summer transfer deadline day in 2004, he was sold to Italian side Juventus for £10.8m. It was alleged he had deliberately injured his Ajax team-mate Rafael van der Vaart during a game between Sweden and Holland.

5 Zlatan became Sweden's Footballer of the Year in 2005. He also picked up that award in 2007 and 2008.

7 Zlatan won two Serie A titles with Juventus – but lost them both because of the match-fixing scandals in Italy.

6 He was Serie A Foreign Footballer of the Year in 2005 and 2008 and was also Serie A Footballer of the Year in 2008.

8 He moved to Inter Milan in August 2006 for £16.7m. His first campaign saw him become Inter's top scorer with 15 goals and his first two seasons both saw him pick up the Serie A title.

9 Zlatan is among the world's best-paid footballers. There have even been reports he may be No.1 in the pay stakes getting around £200,000 a week!

10 The Swede, who has been linked with moves to Arsenal, Chelsea and Real Madrid, has said that he wants to finish his career playing Italy – despite rumours that he could go back to Sweden!

Zlatan
Ibrahimovich

Words of

SOME PLAYERS – and managers - often say things they wish they hadn't! At least they give us a laugh...

"I had 78 attempts and did not manage to hit it once. My excuse is that I don't spend any time in pubs because I am a professional."

Peter Crouch explains away why he couldn't hit the bull in Soccer AM's darts challenge.

"The clean-sheet record is unbelievable. Edwin deserves it. He works a lot for his age!"

Ouch! Cristiano Ronaldo will be buying keeper Edwin van der Sar a zimmer frame next!

"It was unbelievable. I was jumping up and down in front of the television. My dogs were going mad thinking: 'what the....."

Injured Michael Dawson went barking mad when his Spurs side grabbed a late equaliser against Arsenal.

"Are we depressed? Oh yes! We are playing in the Premier League, heading to Chelsea for a glamour game and going to Dubai for some warm weather training. Terrible, isn't it?"

Hull skipper Ian Ashbee sees the bright side despite a run of 15 games that brought City just one win.

wisdom

"The Man City thing is crazy. These guys have all the oil and they can get the money back just by sticking the price of a barrel up a few pence here and there."

If Rio Ferdinand drove a smaller car maybe he wouldn't fuel the buying powers of Man United's biggest rivals...

"We are not brave enough in battle. I think we need to be soldiers. We have to be warriors."

Arsenal defender William Gallas remembers he used to be in the French army!

"Ronaldo is not fit to lace George Best's boots. If Ronaldo was playing 30 years ago he would have been smashed to pieces. He drives me insane with his whining."

Tough guy actor Ray Winstone, a devoted West Ham supporter, gives Cristiano a right old hammering!

"We have five games left, three at home and three away."

Northern Ireland boss Nigel Worthington wasn't good with maths at school.

"He's cocky and arrogant but show him a goal and he's away, like a wind-up toy."

Harry Redknapp reckons Jermain Defoe can score like clockwork.

Know your football

Who am I?

Can you match these overseas players to their rather long real names?

 **Deco**

Kaka

 **Denilson**

Nani

 **Jo**

Robinho

1. Luís Carlos Almeida da Cunha
2. Robson de Souza
3. Ricardo Izecson dos Santos Leite
4. João Alves de Assis Silva
5. Denílson Pereira Neves
6. Anderson Luís de Souza

Match the teams

We've got a few team names jumbled up. Can you sort them out?

1. West Ham Rovers
2. Blackburn United
3. Plymouth Albion
4. Brighton Argyle
5. West Brom United
6. Ipswich City

A Billy Wright STAND

B

D

C umbro.com HOSPITALITY 982 4450

E

NO PLACE LIKE HOME

We want you to match the names of the grounds to the teams who play there. We also want you to match the pictures of the grounds to their clubs.

Nottingham Forest
Picture ___ Ground ___

Blackburn Rovers
Picture ___ Ground ___

Newcastle United
Picture ___ Ground ___

Derby County
Picture ___ Ground ___

Wolves
Picture ___ Ground ___

West Ham
Picture ___ Ground ___

1 St. James' Park
2 Ewood Park
3 Molineux
4 City Ground
5 Pride Park
6 Upton Park

F

my word!

The books your favourite footie stars are reading

Many leading football stars love nothing better than getting their heads stuck into a good book! In fact, every Premier League side has a Reading Champion whose job it is to let youngsters and adults know what fun reading can be. Each champion selects a favourite children's or adults' book. Here are just a few of the favourite books and what the players think of reading!

Bacary Sagna, defender

THE SOUL OF A BUTTERFLY BY MUHAMMAD ALI

"I love this book as it's a spiritual journey of one of my heroes' lives. This book isn't just the life of a sportsman in the ring, it has some valuable lessons and some touching insights. Written with help from his daughter Hana for a personal touch."

Brad Friedel, keeper

STICK MAN BY JULIA DONALDSON

"Julia Donaldson books are just fantastic. The Gruffalo was a book my kids loved and anything they love, I love too. Her rhymes are so clever and the story is so funny - it's one of the best children's books I've seen!"

Paul Robinson, keeper

THE MONK WHO SOLD HIS FERRARI BY ROBIN S. SHARMA

"An extraordinary book that you will not be able to put down once you start it. I bought the book as a present for people and they have all loved it. Inspiring and even life-changing is the only way to describe it."

Jussi Jaaskelainen, keeper

HOW TO SPEAK DRAGONESE BY CRESSIDA COWELL

"How to Speak Dragonese and The Magic Tree House: Castle of Mystery by Mary Pope Osborne are big favourites of my children. We spend a lot of time as a family reading and relaxing. How to Speak Dragonese is full of jokes that always make my boys laugh. Reading is an excellent way to relax."

Henrique Hilario, keeper

BLACK AND BLUE BY PAUL CANOVILLE

"I always enjoy reading books about sport but this book is a little bit different. Paul was the first black player for Chelsea FC and he outlines the difficulties he faced on and off the pitch."

Carlo Nash, keeper

Mark Schwarzer, keeper

LUXURY BACKPACKERS: GLOBAL ADVENTURES IN STYLE BY JILL NASH AND CARLO NASH

"It's important to encourage children to read. They need to know from an early age that reading books can be enjoyable and not just a learning tool. The Roald Dahl books are perfect for children, I've read them all! As for Luxury Backpacking, that's a book written by myself and my wife and we had a brilliant time doing it."

SCARVES, SOMBREROS AND PENALTY SHOOT OUTS

"Scarves & Sombreros is a book I've co-written and it's the second of a five-book series. From my point of view it's a great book based on football. It's based on a lot of our experiences as kids growing up in Australia. It's about an English kid who emigrates from the UK to Australia and I think a lot of people can relate to it because it's based on football, how you fit into society, stick together, form friendships and go through the trials and tribulations of everyday life."

Boaz Myhill, keeper

LORD OF THE FLIES BY WILLIAM GOLDING

"I first read Lord of the Flies as a child and have never forgotten the story. It is incredibly well written and is a gripping read. The issues the book raises about social interaction and the primitive nature of human behaviour are fascinating."

Jamie Carragher, defender

WAR HORSE BY MICHAEL MORPURGO

"War Horse is a brilliant children's book all about the First World War. Reading is something that is so important in all our lives, I hope my being a Premier League Reading Star can encourage young Liverpool fans everywhere to read more."

Daniel Sturridge, striker

PELE: THE AUTOBIOGRAPHY BY PELE

"I enjoy reading factual books rather than fiction and no autobiography can be more inspiring to a young footballer than Pele's. We have a lot of time to kill travelling to away games and reading a story such as his is a great way to pass the time."

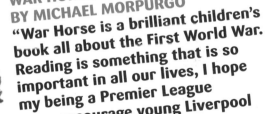

Reading stars by numbers

99 Premier League players have acted as Reading Stars

11 Reading Stars in 2009 are keepers

1 Roald Dahl title has been selected ever year

7 years since the scheme began

15,000 -plus books have been read on the scheme

Wayne Rooney, striker

HARRY POTTER AND THE PHILOSOPHER'S STONE BY JK ROWLING

"Harry Potter is almost every child's favourite book and the same goes for a lot of adults too! JK Rowling is a fantastic author and I would encourage any child to read the Harry Potter books; they are full of excitement and adventure and they really get your imagination going."

Ross Turnbull, keeper

BLESSED BY GEORGE BEST

"Blessed by George Best is an excellent read especially to a footballer like myself. This book allowed me to understand how he lived his life and how his control was taken away from him by alcohol that lead him to end his career early. I enjoy sporting autobiographies as well as sport psychology books as they are topics I am familiar with and ones that I enjoy."

Steven Taylor, defender

FRIENDLY MATCHES BY ALLAN AHLBERG

"The two books I have chosen are, for children, Allan Ahlberg's Friendly Matches' which is packed with great poems and verses about youngsters playing football, and for adults, Bobby Robson My Kind of Toon. Sir Bobby gave me my Newcastle United debut in 2004 and I have a great deal to thank him for. The book is not just about football but the City of Newcastle upon Tyne too and it's a great read."

Danny Higginbotham, defender

A QUIET BELIEF IN ANGELS BY R.J. ELLORY

"I picked up this book almost by chance and was completely surprised by how hooked I became. It's a very dark and haunting story and I honestly couldn't put it down. The book is extremely well written and it really made me think. Some books stick with you and this is definitely one of those!"

David James, keeper

MONEYBALL BY MITCHELL LEWIS

"For someone who knows nothing about baseball this is a compelling insight into an alternative selection process. Just remember whilst reading the book is about Billy Bean and not Billy Bean's book."

Craig Gordon, keeper

**HEAD ON: BOTHAM
THE AUTOBIOGRAPHY
BY IAN BOTHAM**

"I do enjoy reading. It's a nice way to relax away from football and there's nothing like a good book to help you escape from everything going on around you. It's a hobby people of all ages can share and enjoy!"

Didier Zokora, midfielder

THE KICK OFF BY DAN FREEDMAN

"Reading is a great way of relaxing and switching off from football. I like to read in French and English so have lots of books to choose from. Any child who loves football as much as I did as a child will love Dan Freedman's The Kick Off."

Chris Brunt, midfielder

JAMES AND THE GIANT PEACH BY ROALD DAHL

"It's one of the first books I can remember reading when I was at Primary School. I read most of the Roald Dahl books but this was my favourite. I've also seen the film but, as is always the case, the book is better."

Robert Green, keeper

THE ILIAD BY HOMER

"Reading is such a big part of all our lives, everyone should try to make a bit of time each day to read more. You should never be scared of a book either, reading classics like Illiad might seem daunting, but if you take your time, they really are interesting to read, and you gain such a lot from trying them."

Emmerson Boyce, defender

WALLACE AND GROMIT: THE BOOTIFUL GAME BY IAN RIMMER

"I love Wallace and Gromit and The Bootiful Game is a really funny cartoon book, all about football with loads of Wallace's crazy inventions! I'd definitely encourage all young football fans to read more - it's such an important life skill and also a great thing to do to relax."

David James

"I truly believe in the power of the Premier League Reading Stars initiative and I am honoured to be the only player to have been involved in every year of the scheme.

"A love of reading is so important at all ages and if footballers can help to inspire young people to read more, then projects like PLRS really can make a difference."

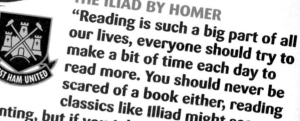

Tongue Twisters!

PUT IT AWAY! It's rude to point or to stick your tongue out at someone. Appears these guys weren't told...

Cristiano Ronaldo

Obafemi Martins

David James

David Bentley

Paul Scholes

Didier Drogba

...and even their bosses are at it!

Wayne Rooney

Arsene Wenger

Jussi Jaaskelainen

Benni McCarthy

Abou Diaby

Martin O'Neill

TOP TRIVIA

YOU CAN BE the most informed anorak around with our pile of footie information!

ROOS ROCKING NOW?

You've got to give him credit for being a good sport – Manchester United striker **WAYNE ROONEY** takes some stick but can dish it out too!

Rooney's missus Coleen asked Noel Gallagher of rock group Oasis if he would sign a guitar for her husband as a birthday present.

Loud mouthed Noel, a massive Manchester City fan, got the expensive vintage guitar off Mrs Rooney and then had it painted blue – the colours of his favourite team.

Then he had the words to Blue Moon, City's supporters' song, written all over the guitar before it was sent back to Wayne.

But he who laughs last... after scoring for United in the Manchester derby Wayne sent a picture to Noel of him and fellow Red Devil Rio Ferdinand celebrating. It contained the message: "To Noel from Spongebob. A great day."

GETTING SHIRTY

They may appear to love him at AC Milan but when it comes to buying **BECKHAM** shirts the Italians are third rate.

When David Beckham moved from Man United to Real Madrid shirts sales at the Bernabeu went through the roof with more than 1,000,000 flying out of the club shop in next to no time.

And when he then moved to LA Galaxy the Americans went potty and shelled out for 250,000 shirts before he even arrived in the USA.

But when Becks arrived in Milan barely 3,000 shirts were sold within the first months of his loan period.

CELEBRITY FANS

RICHARD ARCHER, the lead singer of trendy rock group Hard-Fi isn't a glory hunter. He follows the fortunes of Brentford, the nearest league club to the group's home town of Staines, near Heathrow.

JAMES RIGHTON, leader of The Klaxons, is a follower of Tottenham and he wants to jam with guitar-playing Spurs defender Vedran Corluka.

HIGH FLYER

JACK CORK couldn't believe it when a helicopter landed just off the training pitch and next to the club canteen – and was even more stunned when rockstar Elton John stepped out.

Cork, son of legendary Wimbledon striker Alan, was on loan from Chelsea at Watford when the singer arrived. Elton, the former Watford chairman, had just come to have a chat with the manager and players.

"To see someone like him who my Mum and Nan absolutely love was weird," said Corky.

BLUES FOR REDS

Russian side SPARTAK MOSCOW revealed that it isn't all caviar and champagne at mega-rich Chelsea.

When the Russians used the Blues super training complex in Surrey they had to put up with plastic chairs, disposable plates and BBQs!

Would you believe it?

Manchester United's France full-back **PATRICE EVRA** served up a lobster ravioli when he appeared on MUTV's cookery show Red Devils Kitchen.

Everton are using the 1,000 scouts who compile electronic game Football Manager to look for new players. The owners of game makers Sports Interactive, **PAUL** and **OLIVER COLLYER,** are both Everton fans.

MIDDLESBROUGH upset their fans when they told them to remain quiet during home games! Fans who were moved to the South East corner in a bid to create more atmosphere upset supporters who were already sitting there because they made so much of a din!

ARMY GAME

Plymouth keeper ROMAIN LARRIEU and Arsenal defender WILLIAM GALLAS were both in the army together.

The two players both did their national service for France and turned out for the army's football team.

A-Z OF FOOTBALL

TEST YOUR KNOWLEDGE OF THE BEAUTIFUL GAME IN OUR QUIZ WITH A DIFFERENCE.

A Is for the team who play at The Emirates Stadium

B Benni McCarthy is a striker for which international side?

C The keeper who left Chelsea to join London rivals Spurs in 2009.

D They are known as the Rams.

"What do you mean I look sheepish!"

E Arsenal's Brazil-born striker who was out of action for a year with a broken leg.

G Goodison Park is home to which Premier League side?

F The side whose chairman owns a posh department store and whose ground is on the banks of the River Thames.

H United, who play at Victoria Park and are the favourite team of Sky Sport's Jeff Stelling

I Sweden winger who plays for Inter Milan? And is one of the world's highest-paid footballers.

J Use this letter twice to find the initials of an England midfielder who began his career at Nottingham Forest.

K Brazil frontman who turned down a world recording-breaking transfer to Man City in January 09.

L Team whose fans sing about a ferry crossing their local river.

M Former Chelsea boss who made a massive impression at Inter Milan.

 They ply their trade in League One and play home games at Brisbane Road.

P Nickname of the South Coast side whose fans ask them to 'play-up'.

Q The Hoops who play at Loftus Road.

N Christian name of son who has followed in the footsteps of his famous father by managing an East Midlands side.

"Is that your natural hair colour?"

R Christian name of the former Wolves striker who went from Spurs to Liverpool and back again in just a few months!

S Full name of the ground where the Black Cats play their home games.

T The international side of Tuncay and Colin Kazim-Richards!

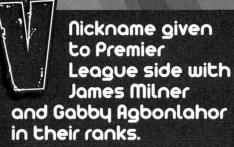

U Name the North London ground where Barnet play.

V Nickname given to Premier League side with James Milner and Gabby Agbonlahor in their ranks.

W England's home games are played at this stadium in North West London.

Y England defender who started at Spurs and is now at Villa.

X Newcastle United's Spain Under-21 striker bought from Deportivo La Coruna.

Z The Italian boss of West Ham United.

10 THINGS YOU NEED TO KNOW ABOUT LIVERPOOL STAR

Dirk Kuyt

1 Dirk Kuyt was born on July 22, 1980, in the seaside town of Katwijk in Holland. He decided to concentrate on football rather than follow his father's profession of fishing.

2 The forward signed professional forms with Dutch First Division outfit Utrecht when he was 18. He stayed there for five years, scoring an average of a goal every three games.

3 Kuyt's hard-working performances and strike rate earned him a £1m move to Feyenoord in 2003. He'd just won the Dutch Cup and become the Netherlands Golden Shoe Winner.

4 During his three years in Rotterdam with Feyenoord he was their top scorer in three successive seasons. That included 36 goals in season 2004-05. The club's captain was named Dutch Footballer of the Year in 2006.

5 A number of Premier League sides were impressed by the 6ft tall striker's goal tally and tracked the Dutchman. Liverpool paid £10m to sign the star in August 2006 and beat off interest from Newcastle United.

6 Ironically, Kuyt scored his first goal for the Reds on his third appearance for them - against Newcastle at Anfield. He made his Premier League debut against West Ham and in the Champions League against Dutch side PSV Eindhoven.

7 The number 18, now often used wide right, wrote himself into Anfield folklore in October 2007 when he hit two penalties in the Merseyside derby at Goodison Park to give Liverpool a last-minute win over Everton.

8 Kuyt made his Holland debut shortly after Euro 2004. He has since appeared in the 2006 World Cup and Euro 2008.

9 Kuyt's first international goal came in a World Cup 2006 qualifier in Macedonia that Holland drew 2-2.

10 He and his wife Gertrude have two children. They run the Dirk Kuyt Foundation for disadvantaged children.

Dirk **Kuyt**

Blasts from the past!

We borrowed Dr Who's Tardis and zoomed back in time to raid through the Shoot picture archives. We came up with a few shots that could leave some players and managers wondering where all the years went! Can you identify these famous faces?

POLICE PUBLIC CALL BOX

F

G

H

I

J

Your answers

A

B

C

D

E

F

G

H

I

J

What's on TV?

WHEN TOP FOOTBALL stars switch off from playing and turn on their televisions what do they watch? Check out our TV guide!

'I wonder what time Eastenders is on?'

'Hey Cowell I can sing a bit too...'

Local heroes

Newcastle defender and England Under-21 captain **STEVEN TAYLOR** is hooked on the X-Factor. And one of the genial Geordie's wishes came true when he met up with judge Simon Cowell. Tayls also admits he tunes in to Tyneside heroes Ant and Dec.

No Bull for Jimmy...

Hull and England midfielder **JIMMY BULLARD** loves the outdoor life and spends most of his free time fishing or playing golf. But when he's stuck indoors the telly's on for Match of the Day or Eastenders - no surprise for a player born in Newham, East London!

'Think I forgot to set the DVD'

Made for Taylor

Veteran Northern Ireland and Birmingham City keeper **MAIK TAYLOR** likes a bit of a laugh when he takes the gloves off. He reckons They Think It's All Over is the most hilarious programme on TV.

'He who dares wins!'

Peckham Plonkers!

Fulham defender **PAUL KONCHESKY** was raised in London so no surprise that he just loves Del and Rodders in Only Fools and Horses. But just like his former England Under-21 team-mate Steve Taylor he never misses X-Factor or Ant and Dec.

Doh!

'I've heard enough, I'm out!'

Homer in

West Ham and England keeper **ROB GREEN** keeps it serious when he is between the sticks but off the pitch he likes nothing better than a good laugh and only watches comedy programmes. Alan Partridge is one of his favourites but he rates The Simpsons as the best show on telly.

The boy Den good...

Hard-man Bolton striker **KEVIN DAVIES** knows he could be nearing the end of his playing days so he gets switched on watching Dragons' Den. He reckons the BBC 2 programme for would-be businessmen might help him to come up with ideas for what to do away from football.

Reality strikes

Aston Villa and England full-back **LUKE YOUNG** admits that he can't ignore any Reality TV on his living room box - even though he knows it will probably be total 'garbage'!

SUPER STEVIE G!

STEVEN GERRARD IS LIVERPOOL! He's likely to finish his career as a one-club man – and he could be one of England's most influential players for quite a number of years yet. We asked people who really know him just how good he is...

> For me Stevie is one of the best players in the world. To say one is the best above anyone else is difficult because there are a lot of quality players about, but he is one of the best. You know when he is on the pitch you have more options to win.

Rafael Benitez, Liverpool boss

> He's one of the best players in the world. I sort of dread going there [Anfield] to play him because he is different class. Gerrard is the heartbeat of the team just like Frank Lampard is with Chelsea.

John Terry, Chelsea and England captain

> It is a fantastic time for him. He is at the top of his game. Steven is important for all the players because he can transmit things and pass on things and inspire players.

Fabio Capello, England coach

> Is he the best in the world? He might not get the attention of Lionel Messi and Ronaldo but yes, I think he just might be. If you don't have a player like Steven Gerrard, who is the engine room, it can affect the whole team."

Zinedine Zidane, France legend

> I'm always happy to play with great players. If you play with someone like Stevie, who is maybe the best player in the world, it can only help you. He is a great passer and he can score goals. He is unbelievable.

Fernando Torres, Anfield team-mate

Let us take you around
THE CLUBS

Arsenal

Arsenal

Season 2008/09

PREMIER LEAGUE: 4th
FA CUP: Semi-final, lost 2-1 to Chelsea
LEAGUE CUP: 5th round, lost 2-0 at Burnley
EUROPE: Champions League semi-final, lost 4-1 to Man United
HIGH POINT: Arshavin's four goals at Liverpool in 4-4 draw
LOW POINT: No trophies – again!

A FEW WORDS WITH... Manuel Almunia

Position: Keeper **Date of birth:** May 19, 1977
Place of birth: Pamplona, Spain
Previous teams: Osasuna, Cartagonova, Sabadell, Celta Vigo, Eiba (loan), Recreativo Huelva (loan), Albacete (loan)

Do you like playing at The Emirates?

"This is Arsenal. This club has thousands of fans and we have to realise to wear an Arsenal shirt is a big honour. You have to be worthy of it."

What's it like being a Premier League player?

"This club gives us everything we need, it's so easy. The only thing that is a bit boring is that we have to spend a lot of time in hotel rooms. But we fly on a private plane and have the best hotels in Europe. Every time we lose we should feel responsible."

How do you rate William Gallas?

"William is a very good professional. When he was captain he would fight for the team. He is a player with more trophies than anyone else in the side and everyone should respect that."

How do Arsenal stay at the top?

"We must look for our identity, the character that gave this club all their titles and trophies. We need to re-find our spirit and desire to win games."

IT'S A FACT!

Almunia is a big collector of World War II memorabilia and often goes to see old black and white films about the campaign

Robin Van Persie

Position: Winger/striker
Date of birth: August 6, 1983
Place of birth: Rotterdam, Holland
Previous teams: Feyenoord

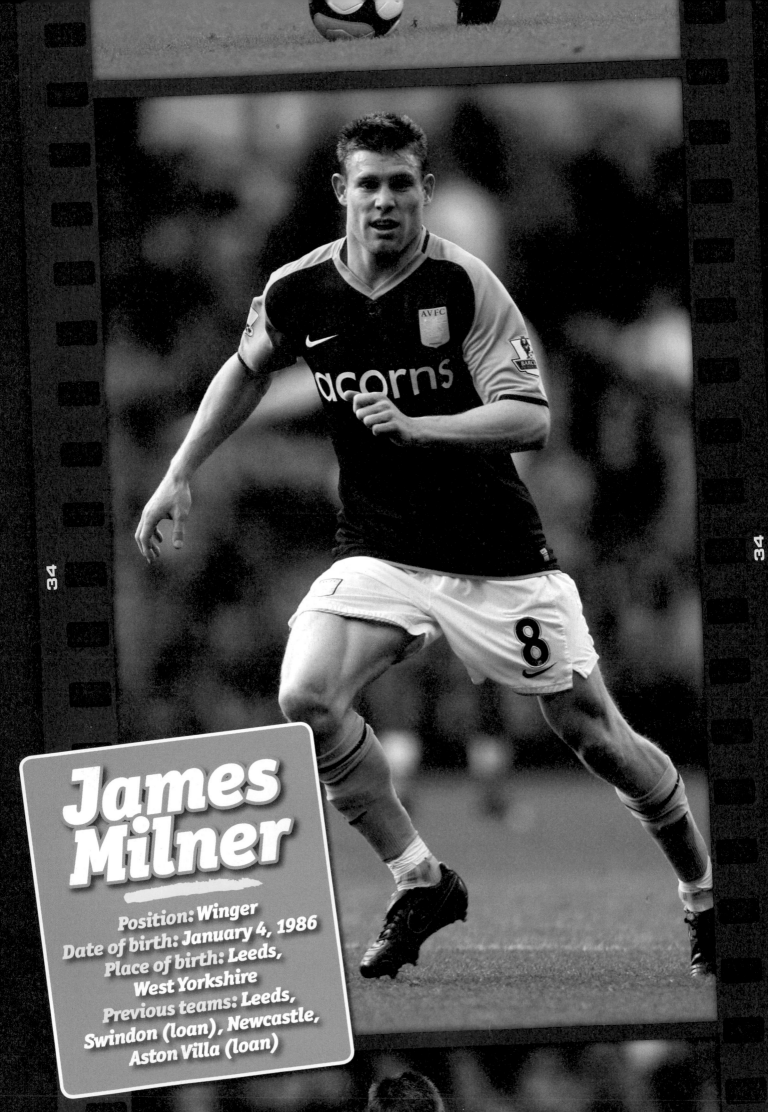

James Milner

Position: Winger
Date of birth: January 4, 1986
Place of birth: Leeds, West Yorkshire
Previous teams: Leeds, Swindon (loan), Newcastle, Aston Villa (loan)

Aston Villa

 A FEW WORDS WITH...

Stiliyan Petrov

Position: Midfielder **Date of birth:** July 5, 1979
Place of birth: Montana, Bulgaria
Previous teams: CSKA Sofia, Celtic

Season 2008/09

PREMIER LEAGUE: 6th
FA CUP: 5th round, lost 3-1 at Everton
LEAGUE CUP: 3rd round, lost 1-0 at home to QPR
EUROPE: UEFA Cup, round of 32, lost 3-1 on aggregate to CSKA Moscow
HIGH POINT: The promise of a bright future with a young squad
LOW POINT: Failing to live up to early season expectations

You got a bit of stick off fans in your early days at Villa...

"When you come off the pitch and see the fans are not happy with your game it is very hard. I had to try and show them they were wrong, that I could play better. I cost a lot of money and I wasn't showing them what I can do."

How did you improve your game and how they felt?

"I come into training every day and try to improve and enjoy myself. The manager was very good to me, I have a lot of respect for him. If you are out of the team you have to fight for your place. I spoke to him and knew I wasn't doing well enough. When he dropped me it was the right thing to do."

Things are much better now though?

"I am happy now when the fans clap me. It's great to hear them chant your name. They now really seem to appreciate what I do."

It wasn't that easy either when you first arrived in Scotland...

"I was 19, confused, and in a strange place where I couldn't communicate. I started at right-back, where I'd never played. It's hard when you don't understand what your team-mates are telling you about where you should be. That made me determined to learn English."

You've signed a new deal at Villa so you must be happy...

"This club wants to move forward every single year. We want to win silverware - some trophies - that's our aim."

IT'S A FACT!

Petrov, who cost an initial £6.5m when he signed for Villa from Celtic in August 2006, scored against Derby with a volley from the half way line. It is thought to be the longest-range strike for the club.

Birmingham City

BIRMINGHAM CITY FOOTBALL CLUB - 1875 -

Season 2008/09

CHAMPIONSHIP: Runners-up
FA CUP: 3rd round, lost 2-0 at home to Wolves
LEAGUE CUP: 2nd round, lost 2-0 at Southampton
EUROPE: n/a
HIGH POINT: Winning 2-1 at Reading on the final day of the Championship season to gain automatic promotion
LOW POINT: Losing in the FA Cup to big rivals Wolves

A FEW WORDS WITH... Kevin Phillips

Position: Striker **Date of birth:** July 25, 1973
Place of birth: Hitchin, Hertfordshire
Previous teams: Watford, Sunderland, Southampton, Aston Villa, West Brom

It must have been great scoring that goal to get City promoted...
"To score the winning goal in the last game of the season to win promotion is great because I hadn't slept all week. Scoring the goal is up there with the other important ones I have got in my career."

Did you think you would win promotion?
"When I first signed for Birmingham, my plan was to try and help them gain promotion and then have a year in the Premier League and see what happens. I'd love to call it a day in the top-flight, but we'll just see what happens."

We gather you had a bit of a tough week personally before the final game...
"I had the worst week of my life, I didn't sleep. I don't know how managers do their job. I'm just a player but the emotions you go through mean you have to enjoy these moments."

You've scored goals wherever you have played. How do you do it?
"There's no secret, really. I'm fortunate to be one of those strikers who knows where the back of the net is. I've always scored goals, ever since I was a young boy, and you never lose that. But it does get harder the older you get and that's why you have to take care of your body. I'm more careful what I eat and drink these days and as long as I feel I can still do a job, I'll keep on playing."

IT'S A FACT!

Super Kev was an outstanding player at Sunderland and one season knocked in 35 goals - the most in one term by a Black Cats player since the Second World War.

35

35

James McFadden

Position: Striker
Date of birth: April 14, 1983
Place of birth: Glasgow
Previous teams: Motherwell, Everton

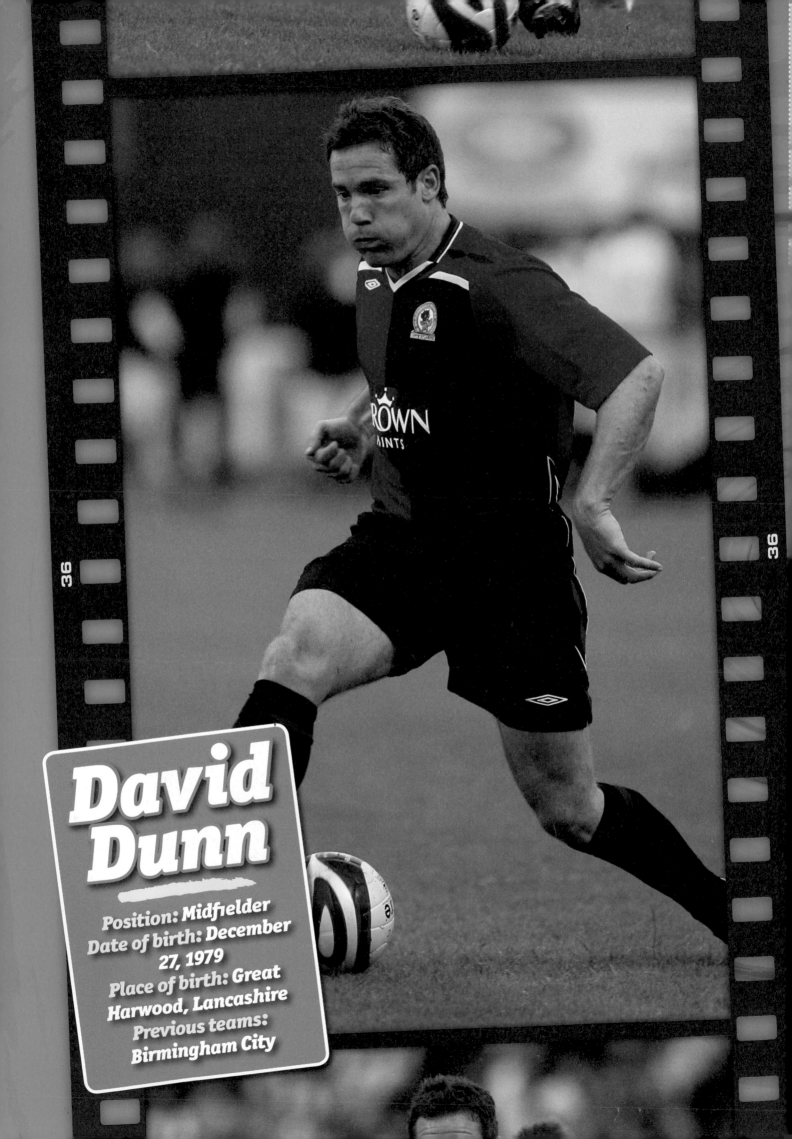

David Dunn

Position: Midfielder
Date of birth: December 27, 1979
Place of birth: Great Harwood, Lancashire
Previous teams: Birmingham City

Blackburn

ARTE ET LABORE

Season 2008/09

PREMIER LEAGUE: 15th
FA CUP: 5th round, lost
1-0 at Coventry
LEAGUE CUP: Quarter-finals,
lost 5-3 at Man United
EUROPE: n/a
HIGH POINT: Appointing Sam
Allardyce as their new boss
LOW POINT: Realising Paul Ince
was not the boss for Rovers

A FEW WORDS WITH....

Ryan Nelsen

Position: Defender Date of birth: October 18, 1977
Place of birth: Christchurch, New Zealand
Previous teams: DC United

What was it like battling away from relegation?
"You do look at the other results. We had to take care of our own business though. You can't lose concentration for a minute in this league."

How important was the appointment of Sam Allardyce?
"Before Sam came in we were a sinking ship, in big trouble. If the directors had not moved when they did we'd have been in serious trouble. Sam changed little things that his experience as a manager saw."

You get lots of info off Big Sam?
"We get all the stats from the games. It tells you how far you've run, how many high-intensity runs you've made and how many balls you've given away."

We gather this has helped keeper Paul Robinson...
"He's been working really hard and made improvements to his lifestyle, strength and speed. It's really starting to tell, you can see it in his game and he has started to show what a great keeper his is."

IT'S A FACT!

Nelsen was an excellent cricket player but decided instead to concentrate on football and played in America's MLS before joining Blackburn in 2005.

Bolton Wanderers

A FEW WORDS WITH... Kevin Davies

Position: Striker **Date of birth:** March 26, 1977
Place of birth: Sheffield
Previous teams: Chesterfield, Southampton, Blackburn, Southampton, Millwall (loan)

Season 2008/09

PREMIER LEAGUE: 13th
FA CUP: 3rd round, lost 2-1 at Sunderland
LEAGUE CUP: 2nd round, lost 2-1 at home to Northampton
EUROPE: n/a
HIGH POINT: No relegation fears
LOW POINT: Losing 4-3 at Chelsea after a comeback from 4-0 down!

You don't appear to have been in the headlines as much for your tackling last season...

"I only got four yellow cards so I'm slacking a bit. I'm not even in the Premier League's dirty dozen! There's physical and there's dirty. I'm a physical player, not a dirty one."

You get a bit of stick too though!

"If you look at the statistics, I'm also the most fouled player in the Premier League. Cristiano Ronaldo says he's sick and tired of getting kicked. Well I've been kicked more times than him but I just get straight back up and get on with it."

So who is your most difficult opponent?

"I always have a good battle against John Terry. I've caught him a couple of times and given him a bloody lip, and he's caught me but that's the way it should be... just get up and get on with the game."

It must have been nice to get that England call-up!

"To be included in the provisional squad was a real boost. You feel you're in the England manager's thoughts, which is great. I'd like to be given the chance to perform at international level and show people what I can do."

Your keeper Jussi Jaaskelainen deserves a lot of praise too...

"Jussi's one of the best keepers in the world. Since I've been at the club he's been amazing and I really can't think of a mistake he's made. He is one of the hardest trainers I've ever worked with. He's in early and will be in the gym before and after training."

IT'S A FACT!

Kevin admits that if he was a manager and had a blank cheque to buy any player in the world he'd probably go out and snatch Wayne Rooney.

Fabrice Muamba

Position: Midfielder
Date of birth: April 6, 1988
Place of birth: DR Congo
Previous teams: Arsenal,
Birmingham City

Chris Eagles

Position: Midfielder
Date of birth:
November 19, 1985
Place of birth: Hemel
Hempstead, Hertfordshire
Previous teams:
Man United, Watford
(loan), Sheff Wed (loan),
NEC Nijmegen (loan)

Burnley

Wade Elliott

**Position: Midfielder Date of birth: December 14, 1978
Place of birth: Southampton
Previous teams: Bournemouth**

Season 2008/09

CHAMPIONSHIP: Play-off winners
FA CUP: 5th round, lost 3-0 at Arsenal
LEAGUE CUP: Semi-finals, lost 6-4 to Spurs (lost away 4-1, won home 3-2)
EUROPE: n/a
HIGH POINTS: Returning to the top-flight for the first time in 33 years – and knocking Chelsea out of the League Cup
LOW POINT: Not making it two Wembley appearances

How did it feel to score the only goal in the Play-off Final?

"I think it took a little while for it to sink in. It's far and away the best goal I'll ever score, probably. It fell nicely, I couldn't really strike it because it was turning a bit and it seemed to take a long time to go in. When it did, I thought about running up to my Mum and Dad but they were in the opposite corner and it was so hot."

You've had a great time since arriving from Bournemouth...

"I enjoy it here. I have improved and progressed as a player and the gaffer is very positive in his approach. He likes to play attacking football and it shows in our performances. Everybody has ambitions to play at the very top level."

And you were Player of the Season two years in a row...

"I was humbled but pleased. Some of the football we have played has been really good and it brings home to you what a good squad we've got. Hopefully there's more to come. I enjoy coming in to work with the lads every day."

Have you always been football fan?

"I used to watch Southampton as a kid, and Matt le Tissier was my hero. I'd just try to strike the ball like he did. Matchdays are the best things - it's rotten if you work all week and aren't involved in the match."

IT'S A FACT!

The 7,000 fans who held season tickets in the Championship were given free 2009-2010 cards by the club for their loyalty. The total cost of the thank you was around £2m.

Chelsea

CHELSEA FOOTBALL CLUB

Season 2008/09

PREMIER LEAGUE: 3rd
FA CUP: Winner, beat Everton 2-1
LEAGUE CUP: 4th round, drew 1-1 at home to Burnley (lost 4-5 on pens)
EUROPE: Champions League semi-finals, lost to Barcelona
HIGH POINT: Lifting the FA Cup
LOW POINT: Losing on away goals rule to Barca after 1-1 at the Bridge

A FEW WORDS WITH...

Joe Cole

Position: Midfielder **Date of birth:** November 8, 1981
Place of birth: Islington, North London
Previous teams: West Ham

After your injury problems – worried about tackles?

"Something has to be done about the really nasty tackles. Everyone likes a hard tackle and I sometimes go in hard myself, but never with the intent to hit someone. A ban is needed that would hurt the player and the team."

What do you feel like when you aren't in the team?

"Naturally people get frustrated when they don't play or get substituted. There would be something wrong if they didn't. It just shows you care and I have always been passionate about my football, that's the way I am."

How difficult is it being a professional footballer?

"Football doesn't stand still. I am competing with other people in the squad and you want to play well. When you join a big club you have to expect competition. I have always thrived on it. I love competing and learning from big players."

You love the Blues, don't you?

"If I was to finish my career at Chelsea, I'd be delighted. The next five years will see the best of me. Hopefully, I will play for a long time because I do not rely on pace. I put my heart and soul into every game. I'd hate to fall out with the supporters or for anything to go wrong."

IT'S A FACT!

Chelsea forked out £6.6m to buy Joe from West Ham in summer 2003. He had come through their famed academy and was appointed club captain at the age of 21.

Michael Essien

Position: Midfielder
Date of birth: December 3, 1982
Place of birth: Ghana
Previous teams: Bastia, Lyon

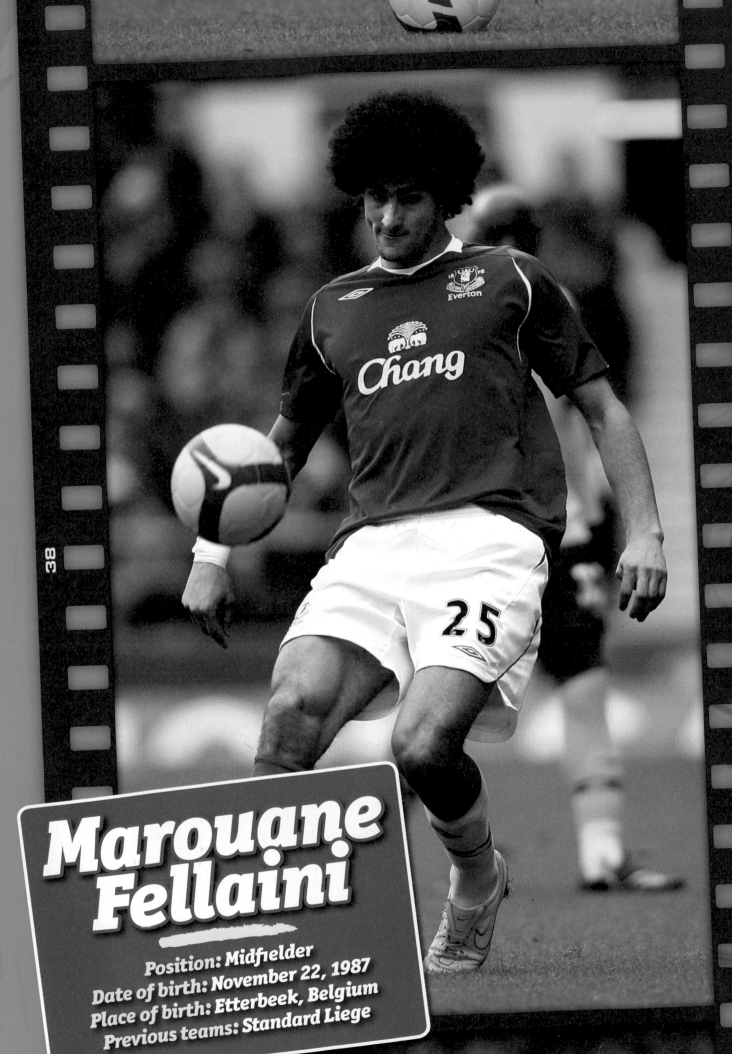

Marouane Fellaini

Position: Midfielder
Date of birth: November 22, 1987
Place of birth: Etterbeek, Belgium
Previous teams: Standard Liege

Everton

18 78

NIL SATIS NISI OPTIMUM

Everton

Season 2008/09

PREMIER LEAGUE: 5th
FA CUP: Final, lost 2-1 to Chelsea
LEAGUE CUP: 3rd round,
lost 1-0 at Blackburn Rovers
EUROPE: UEFA Cup 1st round, lost
4-3 to Standard Liege (2-2, 2-1)
HIGH POINT: Finishing just
behind the Big Four
LOW POINT: Going out of
Europe at the first hurdle

A FEW WORDS WITH...

Tim Cahill

Position: Midfielder **Date of birth:** December 6, 1979
Place of birth: Sydney, Australia
Previous teams: Sydney, Millwall

Are you going to finish your career at Goodison Park?

"Everyone knows I am fiercely proud of my roots and that perhaps one day I may play club football back home. But to say I will be doing it at the end of my current deal [2012] is simply not true. When my contract expires I would hope that I still have a few more years left at this level."

What do you think of English football?

"The English Premier League is the best in the world and I have absolutely no plans to move. Tactics is something I've loved learning about since coming to the Premier League. It can get a bit repetitive sometimes, standing around outside doing corners and throw-ins again and again."

Your FA Cup goal against Villa in 2008 was something special...

"That was for the victims of the fires back home. When I went back I saw the effect it had, and all of us in the Australia squad were talking about it, it was so devastating. It puts everything in perspective and I was just happy I was able to contribute something with the goal and the gesture."

IT'S A FACT!

Marouane Fellaini cost Everton a club record £15m, also a best for a Belgian transfer, when he signed in 2008. There had also been interest from Aston Villa and Tottenham

Fulham

Mark Schwarzer

Position: Keeper **Date of birth:** October 6, 1972
Place of birth: Sydney, Australia
Previous teams: Kaiserslautern, Bradford City, Middlesbrough

Season 2008/09

PREMIER LEAGUE: 7th
FA CUP: Quarter-finals, lost 4-0, home to Man United
LEAGUE CUP: Third round, lost 1-0 at Burnley
EUROPE: n/a
HIGH POINT: Qualifying for Europe
LOW POINT: Wondering if a Europa League adventure could be a problem with a small squad!

Was it difficult leaving Boro after more than ten years?

"I felt the time was right for me to move on, and when the opportunity to talk to [manager] Roy Hodgson came, although I had other offers from some great clubs throughout Europe, it didn't take long to make a decision about joining Fulham."

Was Hodgson the main reason you joined?

"It's fantastic to have that type of manager who encourages you and gives you self-belief, so that if you make a mistake you just get your head down and rectify it."

Fulham had a good season...

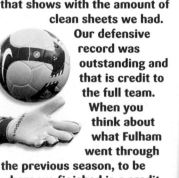

"From the front line to the back line we defended as a team and that shows with the amount of clean sheets we had. Our defensive record was outstanding and that is credit to the full team. When you think about what Fulham went through the previous season, to be where we finished is a credit to everyone at the club."

How long will you keep playing for Oz?

"I haven't really put a time frame on it. My main aim was to qualify for the World Cup. You've got to set yourself high standards."

IT'S A FACT!

Mark is one of only eight players to pass the 60-cap mark for Australia. He is his country's longest-serving current player having made his debut in 1993.

Aaron Hughes

Position: Defender
Date of birth: November 8, 1979
Place of birth: Cookstown, Northern Ireland
Previous teams: Newcastle United, Aston Villa

Hull City

HULL CITY A.F.C.

'THE TIGERS'

Season 2008/09

PREMIER LEAGUE: 17th

FA CUP: Quarter-final, lost 2-1 at Arsenal

LEAGUE CUP: 2nd round, lost 2-1 at Swansea aet

EUROPE: n/a

HIGH POINT: Four league wins in a row - at Arsenal and Spurs, home to West Ham and then at West Brom.

LOW POINT: Boss Phil Brown singing at the final game of the season!

A FEW WORDS WITH... Michael Turner

Position: Defender **Date of birth:** November 9, 1983
Place of birth: Lewisham, South London
Previous teams: Charlton Athletic, Leyton Orient (loan), Brentford

Happy at Hull?
"Early last season I signed a four-year deal and that says it all. I was desperate for the club to stay up and having done that it's a great achievement. This club wants to really push on from here and become an established Premier League side and I want to be part of that."

What was your first year like in the Premier League?
"A few people raised their eyebrows as to whether I could perform at this level. I'd like to think that I've progressed gradually throughout the season. All I have tried to do is be a consistent performer every week."

Was it difficult during the bad runs?
"Spirits were good, but they always have been. Everyone worked hard to try to get away from the bottom three. It has been a dream playing against some of the best teams in the world and at the best stadiums and I want to do that for a long time."

What was the major problem?
"We did well in games but gave away goals at crucial times, especially just before half-time."

IT'S A FACT!

Michael was boss Phil Brown's first signing and the £350,000 fee - a Tigers record for a defender - now looks like a bargain.

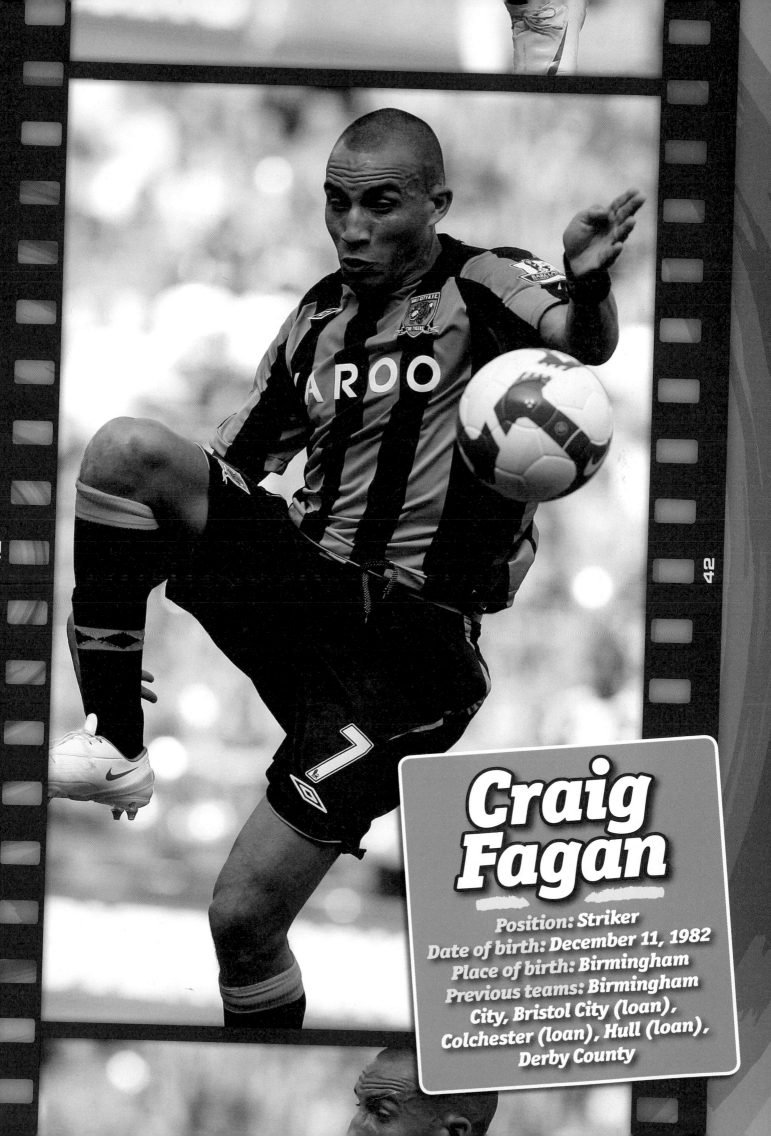

Craig Fagan

Position: Striker
Date of birth: December 11, 1982
Place of birth: Birmingham
Previous teams: Birmingham City, Bristol City (loan), Colchester (loan), Hull (loan), Derby County

Liverpool

YOU'LL NEVER WALK ALONE

LIVERPOOL FOOTBALL CLUB

EST·1892®

Season 2008/09

PREMIER LEAGUE: 2nd
FA CUP: 4th round,
lost 1-0 at Everton (replay)
LEAGUE CUP: 4th round,
lost 4-2 at Tottenham
EUROPE: Champions League quarter-finals, lost 7-5 to Chelsea (1-3, 4-4)
HIGH POINT: Beating Real Madrid
LOW POINT: Going close but not winning any silverware

A FEW WORDS WITH...

Fernando Torres

Position: Striker **Date of birth:** March 20, 1984
Place of birth: Fuenlabrada, Madrid
Previous teams: Atletico Madrid

What's Rafa Benitez like?
"The manager is good and strong and he has all our support and we are with him all the way. The manager can compete with anyone, he proved that in Spain. Rafa is more English that Spanish. He learns a lot every day."

What's it like being a Premier League player?
"Football in England is something else and that applies to training as well. We go flat out from start to finish. It's great and one of the reasons I wanted to join Liverpool."

How did you cope when you arrived on Merseyside?
"I fell in love with Liverpool on my first day. There were 100 people at the airport when I got my passport checked and they applauded me and gave me a guard of honour."

What was life like in Spain?
"After being part of Atletico Madrid for so long they are a club in my heart. That means I could never sign for Real Madrid. Every striker has a club he finds it easy to score against. For some reason mine seemed to be Barcelona."

IT'S A FACT!

Fernando fancies himself as a bit of a rock star and even appeared on stage with Spanish pop group El Canto del Loco. His friend Dani Martin is lead singer and Nando played guitar for him!

Steven Gerrard

Position: Midfielder
Date of birth: May 30, 1980
Place of birth:
Whiston, Merseyside
Previous teams: Liverpool
from trainee

Vincent Kompany

Position: Midfielder
Date of birth: April 10, 1986
Place of birth: Ukkle, Belgium
Previous teams: Anderlecht, Hamburg

Manchester City

M.C.F.C.

Superbia In Proelio

Season 2008/09

PREMIER LEAGUE: 10th
FA CUP: 3rd round, lost 3-0 at home to Nottingham Forest
LEAGUE CUP: 2nd round, drew 2-2 at Brighton (lost 5-3 on pens)
EUROPE: UEFA Cup, quarter-final, lost 4-3 to Hamburg
HIGH POINT: The stunning form of Stephen Ireland
LOW POINT: Hit and miss Robinho

A FEW WORDS WITH... Stephen Ireland

Position: Midfielder **Date of birth:** August 22, 1986
Place of birth: Cork, Republic of Ireland
Previous teams: Academy graduate

How good a signing was Craig Bellamy?

"Craig's a fiery person who always wants to win. You can see why the gaffer signed him. He's a proper winner who plays with his heart on his sleeve. As soon as you get the ball you look for him because his movement is brilliant."

How do you approach games?

"I go into every game with the mentality that I want to win for myself, the team and the gaffer. You are not going to win in the Premier League unless you work hard. I would love to keep scoring. I have set myself targets and just want to keep reaching them."

Are you happy at City?

"I'd love to stay here for a long time and for the club to show me they are serious about me as I am about them. I want to concentrate on football and just keep going."

Are you worried when City buy big-name players?

"That's what's so good about the club going out and bringing in world-class players, it forces everyone else to improve. I've always tried to work on my consistency and being surrounded by great players is a help. I have to be on top of my game, because if I was to get dropped I might be out for six or seven matches."

IT'S A FACT!

Stephen played junior football for Cobh Rovers in Ireland – the first team of former Republic captain Roy Keane. Keano tried to buy Ireland when he was manager at Sunderland.

Manchester United

Season 2008/09

PREMIER LEAGUE: Champions
FA CUP: Semi-finals, lost to Everton (0-0 after extra time, 4-2 on pens,)
LEAGUE CUP: Winners, beat Tottenham 4-1 on pens (0-0 after aet)
EUROPE: Champions League Final, lost 2-0 to Barcelona in Rome
HIGH POINT: Winning a record third Premier League title in a row
LOW POINT: Losing in Rome

A FEW WORDS WITH... Ben Foster

Position: Keeper **Date of birth:** April 3, 1983
Place of birth: Leamington Spa, Warwickshire
Previous teams: Stoke City, Bristol City (loan), Tiverton Town (loan), Stafford Rangers (loan), Kidderminster (loan), Wrexham (loan), Watford (loan).

What's it like at Old Trafford

"You've only got one chance at being at United and there have been plenty of players in the past who maybe jumped ship too early. I'm going to give it my all and force my way in."

Did you benefit from being loaned to Watford?

"It was massive. It brought my game on tenfold and was everything I could have wanted. When I signed we were expected to get relegated and we ended up getting promoted through the play-offs, which was a great feeling and definitely the best way to get promoted. Plus I got Premiership experience under my belt."

Is there a big quality gap between the Championship and Premier League?

"The main difference is the speed of the game and the pace of the players you are playing against. If a defender in front of you slips up you know he's not going to get back in time to make a tackle and that means the opposition are in and going to score. Also the way players in the Premiership put the ball into the box, they don't just pump it into the air, they whip it in with absolute conviction. It's a massive difference in quality."

What are your strengths as a player?

"I think probably commanding my area and coming out for crosses. I'm not a bad shot-stopper and I think distribution is a big part of my game as well as communication and bossing my back four."

IT'S A FACT!

Ben hadn't even played a first-team game for Stoke when Sir Alex Ferguson spotted him out on loan at other clubs and agreed a £1m deal to take him to Old Trafford.

Michael Carrick

Position: Midfielder
Date of birth: July 28, 1981
Place of birth:
Wallsend, Newcastle
Previous teams: West Ham,
Swindon (loan), Birmingham
City (loan), Tottenham

Portsmouth

Portsmouth F.C.

Season 2008/09

PREMIER LEAGUE: 14th
FA CUP: 4th round,
lost 2-0 home to Swansea
LEAGUE CUP: 3rd round,
lost 4-0 home to Chelsea
EUROPE: UEFA Cup group stage
HIGH POINT: Beating the drop
LOW POINT: No Harry Redknapp

A FEW WORDS WITH...

David James

Position: Keeper **Date of birth:** August 1, 1970
Place of birth: Welwyn, Hertfordshire
Previous teams: Watford, Liverpool, Aston Villa,
West Ham, Manchester City

You're 39 – any thoughts on your international career?

"I'll never give up on playing for my country, but there will come a point when some people will wish I would. I hope my journey isn't finished yet. There are a lot of people who finish their career far too early. I don't intend to finish until I have fulfilled all my dreams."

You are still hooked on football then?

"I love this game so much and every milestone leads to another milestone. This is one of the best [England] squads I have been involved with and I feel I could go on all the way, we are so good together."

And you set a new Premier League appearance record when you passed 536 games in 2009...

"To reach that landmark was a huge personal achievement and hopefully I can keep going for a while yet. I was very proud to receive a merit award from Barclays in recognition for all the hard work I've put in over the past 17 years. I am playing in the best domestic league in the world so if you can play in it for that long it must say something."

Is the game more difficult today?

"People talk about the number of games players face these days, but we have bigger squads and professionals to turn to for advice about training - doctors and physios to advise us on how best to prepare for our next match. I'm sure it wasn't like that in the mid-1970s."

IT'S A FACT!

Jamo loves collecting things and besides a whole load of back numbers of Shoot magazine he had a load of Chopper bikes from the 1970s.

Peter Crouch

Position: Striker
Date of birth: January 30, 1981
Place of birth:
Macclesfield, Cheshire
Previous teams: Tottenham,
QPR, Portsmouth, Aston Villa,
Norwich city (loan),
Southampton, Liverpool

Stoke City

STOKE CITY · 1863 · THE POTTERS

Season 2008/09

PREMIER LEAGUE: 12th
FA CUP: 3rd round, lost 2-0 at Hartlepool
LEAGUE CUP: 5th round, lost 1-0 home to Derby
EUROPE: n/a
HIGH POINT: Staying up!
LOW POINT: 5-0 loss at Man United

A FEW WORDS WITH Matthew Etherington

Position: Midfielder **Date of birth:** August 14, 1981
Place of birth: Truro, Cornwall
Previous teams: Peterborough, Tottenham, Bradford City (loan), West Ham

What made you join Stoke?

"It was the right time to come here and chill out and concentrate on football. I'm settled and happy as a person and it is different to the bright lights of London."

But aren't you a bigger star here?

"In London you can go out and not be recognized but that doesn't happen in Stoke. Fans come up to me in Tesco and thank me for coming here, that's really nice."

Do you go back to the capital?

"I do go back occasionally for lunch with some of the West Ham lads and I also have a lot of family and friends in London who I see too."

Weren't you worried about relegation?

"My friends told me we would be relegated and we would struggle. But the manager told us we got where we are because of hard work and we had to keep fighting to cross the winning line."

IT'S A FACT!

Former England Under-21 winger Matthew and Welshman Simon Davies both left Peterborough for Spurs at the same time in a joint deal. Davies has since moved on to Everton and Fulham.

James Beattie

Position: Striker
Date of birth: February 27, 1978
Place of birth: Lancaster
Previous teams: Blackburn, Southampton, Everton, Sheffield United

Sunderland

SUNDERLAND A.F.C

A FEW WORDS WITH... Kenwyne Jones

Position: Striker **Date of birth:** October 5, 1984
Place of birth: Trinidad and Tobago
Previous teams: Southampton, Sheffield Wednesday (loan), Stoke City (loan)

Season 2008/09

PREMIER LEAGUE: 16th
FA CUP: 4th round, lost 2-1 at Blackburn in a replay
LEAGUE CUP: 4th round, lost 2-1, home to Blackburn
EUROPE: n/a
HIGH POINT: Retaining Premier League status despite the last day defeat to Chelsea
LOW POINT: Losing 4-1 at home to Bolton

Is it true you once trained with Man United?
"I had a trial there years ago. It was my first experience of a big club and their set up. When I experienced what it was like I knew this is what I wanted to do. It spurred me on to get there."

Happy how you have progressed since then?
"Where I am now is where I'm supposed to be. I can't say Man United made a mistake. I went all over the place, but I never gave up."

You have even been likened to Didier Drogba..
"The Drogba comparison is one I have heard and it's nice to be mentioned with someone like that but I have to forge my own way. It's good others have talked about me and noticed what I have done. When Roy Keane [former manager] said I was the best striker in the Premier League and worth £40m the only thing that I could do was smile."

So what's the plan now?
"I believe I need to improve every part of my game. The perception is that we are all laid back in the Caribbean because there is a different outlook on life but we can be busy when it matters."

IT'S A FACT!

Jonesy travelled to Europe to find a football club who would give him a contract so he didn't have to join his country's army.

Nyron Nosworthy

Position: Defender
Date of birth: October 11, 1980
Place of birth: Brixton, South London
Previous teams: Gillingham

Tottenham

Jermain Defoe

Position: Striker **Date of birth:** October 7, 1982
Place of birth: Beckton, East London
Previous teams: West Ham, Bournemouth (loan), Tottenham, Portsmouth

Season 2008/09

PREMIER LEAGUE: 8th
FA CUP: 4th round, lost 2-1 at Man United
LEAGUE CUP: Finalists, beaten 4-1 on pens by Man United (0-0 aet)
EUROPE: UEFA Cup last 32, lost 3-1 to Shakhtar Donetsk (2-0, 1-1)
HIGH POINT: Appointing Harry Redknapp as manager
LOW POINT: Losing 5-2 at Man United after leading 2-0

You appear to be in Fabio Capello's good books...

"When a new manager comes in everyone is equal and fights for their places. Players come in and do a good job. As a player it helps when the manager shows faith. When I saw my name on the team sheet I was delighted."

What's it like being a professional footballer?

"A lot of people say that a footballer's life is easy. It's not easy at all, it's hard and you have to be very dedicated. There are a lot of sacrifices you have to make, especially when all of your friends are going out drinking and you are stuck at home watching Match of the Day or relaxing before games. But it's worth it in the end."

How do you feel about scoring?

"It's normal to want to win the Golden Boot, most strikers do. When I go home after a game I always look at the top scorers charts on the TV and see where I am."

How much did you benefit from your loan as a youngster?

"I think it is important for young players to go out on loan. I was getting a few games in the reserves at West Ham, a few spots on the bench for the first-team, but I am really glad I went to Bournemouth for the experience. I really enjoyed it. When you play games you feel so much sharper."

IT'S A FACT!

Jermain has played under Harry Redknapp three times - at West Ham, Portsmouth and now Spurs. Bournemouth - the club where he went on loan - were once managed by Redknapp!

Robbie Keane

Position: Striker
Date of birth: July 8, 1980
Place of birth: Dublin
Previous teams: Wolves, Coventry, Inter Milan, Leeds, Tottenham, Liverpool

West Ham United

WEST HAM UNITED

Season 2008/09

PREMIER LEAGUE: 9th
FA CUP: 5th round, lost 2-0 in replay at Middlesbrough
LEAGUE CUP: 3rd round, lost 1-0 at Watford
EUROPE: n/a
HIGH POINT: Appointing Zola boss
LOW POINT: Two league defeats and FA Cup exit in a grim February

A FEW WORDS WITH... Scott Parker

Position: Midfielder **Date of birth:** October 13, 1980
Place of birth: Lambeth, South London
Previous teams: Charlton, Norwich (loan), Chelsea, Newcastle

Your appearance in a McDonalds ad when you were a youngster just wont go away?
"I hear it's still on YouTube and my son has seen it a few times. I hope I will be remembered more for what I have done on the pitch rather than the advert."

Does boss Gianfranco Zola tell you much about when he was a player?
"He keeps reminding us of what he has done! We don't give him any stick though. We just let him get on with it."

The Hammers turned down a big transfer bid from Manchester City for you in January...
"They told me about it and said they didn't want the deal to happen. There are great plans here and I want to be part of them."

What about playing for England again?
"Every kid wants to play for their country and I was no different. I know there are good players in my position but I will try to force my way into the squad. If you play good football and stay injury-free you have a chance. I gather Fabio Capello watches our club more than any other."

IT'S A FACT!

Scotty has cost a total of £23.5m in transfer fees – £10m to Chelsea, £6.5m to Newcastle and £7m to West Ham.

Carlton Cole

Position: Striker
Date of birth: November 12, 1983
Place of birth: Croydon, Surrey
Previous teams: Chelsea,
Wolves (loan), Charlton (loan),
Aston Villa (loan)

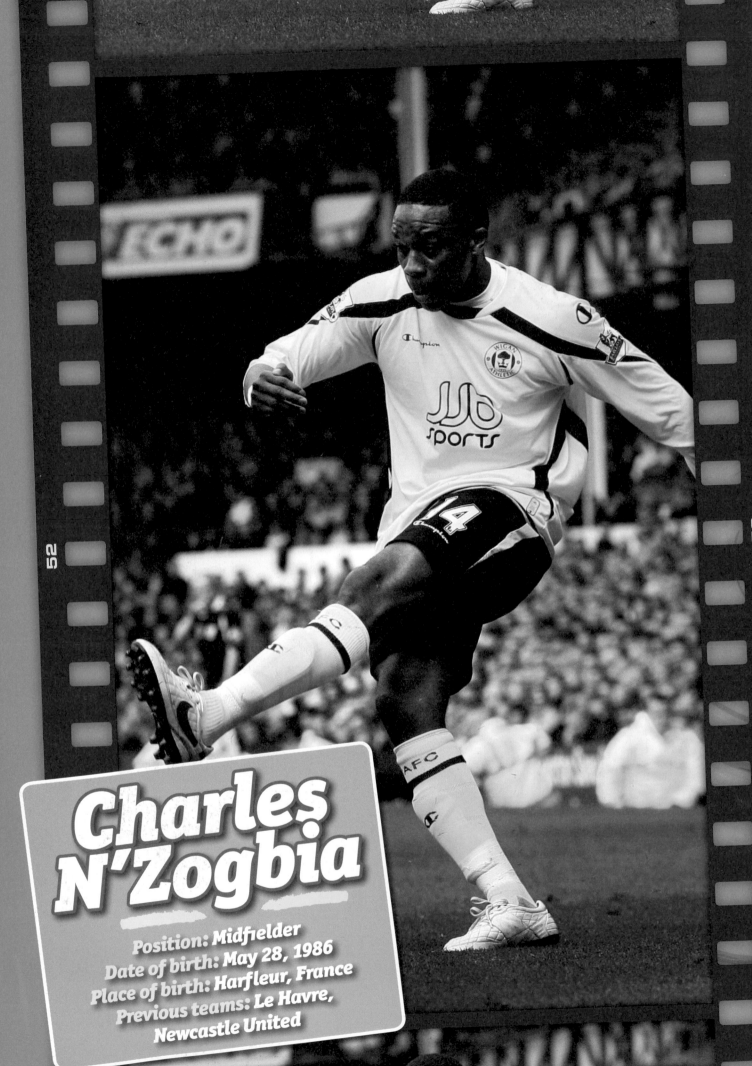

Charles N'Zogbia

Position: Midfielder
Date of birth: May 28, 1986
Place of birth: Harfleur, France
Previous teams: Le Havre, Newcastle United

Wigan Athletic

Season 2008/09

PREMIER LEAGUE: 11th
FA CUP: 3rd round, lost 3-1 at Tottenham
LEAGUE CUP: 4th round, lost 3-0 at Arsenal
EUROPE: n/a
HIGH POINT: The 5-0 home victory over Hull City
LOW POINT: Grim October and April which saw seven defeats!

A FEW WORDS WITH Lee Cattermole

Position: Midfielder **Date of birth:** March 21, 1988
Place of birth: Stockton-on-Tees, Cleveland
Previous teams: Middlesbrough

What's your favourite position?
"I prefer to play in the centre of midfield. I've played there my entire career, all the way through the youth ranks with Boro and into the first-team. I feel comfortable there. Sometimes I lose my strength as a ball-winner if I play on the right."

You've got a bit of a reputation as a battler...
"I always give my all and I don't like losing. In fact, I hate losing. You've got to play with passion and spirit and I will always roll up my sleeves and give it a good go. Where it comes from, I just don't know."

Time's on your side to progress your career further too...
"People forget how young I am sometimes. We played Arsenal in the Carling Cup and everyone was talking about all these great kids and what great futures they have. And yet a lot of them were only my age. I've been playing in the Premier League since I was 17. Nobody thinks of me as one of the young lads any more and I'd rather it be like that."

You have said former Boro captain George Boateng was a major influence...
"He's a really good player and I have always looked up to him. The more games you play the more it helps your confidence. George helped me with that, too, and I became more mature as a person thanks to him."

And you have admiration for Steven Gerrard...
"If I'm as successful as Mr Gerrard, I'll be very happy! He's a great role model."

IT'S A FACT!
Catts was Middlesbrough's youngest-ever captain, at the age of 18 years and 47 days. He has also been skipper of England Under-19s.

Wolverhampton Wanderers

A FEW WORDS WITH... Andy Keogh

Position: Striker **Date of birth:** May 16, 1986
Place of birth: Dublin
Previous teams: Leeds United, Scunthorpe (loan), Bury (loan) Scunthorpe

Season 2008/09

CHAMPIONSHIP: Champions
FA CUP: 4th round, lost 2-1 home to Middlesbrough
LEAGUE CUP: 2nd round, lost on penalties to Rotherham (0-0 aet)
EUROPE: n/a
HIGH POINT: Winning 1-0 against QPR to seal promotion at home
LOW POINT: No wins in February

Wolves were pretty hot last season!
"We had such a great team spirit and we didn't want to break that up, because we're such good friends on and off the pitch. Sometimes things don't go our way, but we stick at it."

And you got a new contract...
"I was delighted to sign the deal. I'm really settled here and am more than happy to have signed on until 2012. I'm still getting better as a player and trying to learn more about the game and this is a great place to keep doing that."

Boss Mick McCarthy will be a bit of a legend now...
"The gaffer has been very good with some signings and I'm sure he'll make some astute ones when he needs to as well. Hopefully I can keep improving and growing as a player with the gaffer's help."

You've won a fan in Ireland boss Giovanni Trapattoni too...
"It's good to know I am in his plans and I just have to keep working as hard as I can to stay in those plans. He's helped me with little things."

So how does he help?
"Sometimes in training you don't have to talk, he just shows you what to do. He's out there with his boots on and will start explaining in English and finish up in Italian."

IT'S A FACT!

Andy, who cost Wolves £850,000 from Scunthorpe, admits that his equaliser for the Republic against Serbia at Croke Park in Trapattoni's first game in charge was a dream come true.

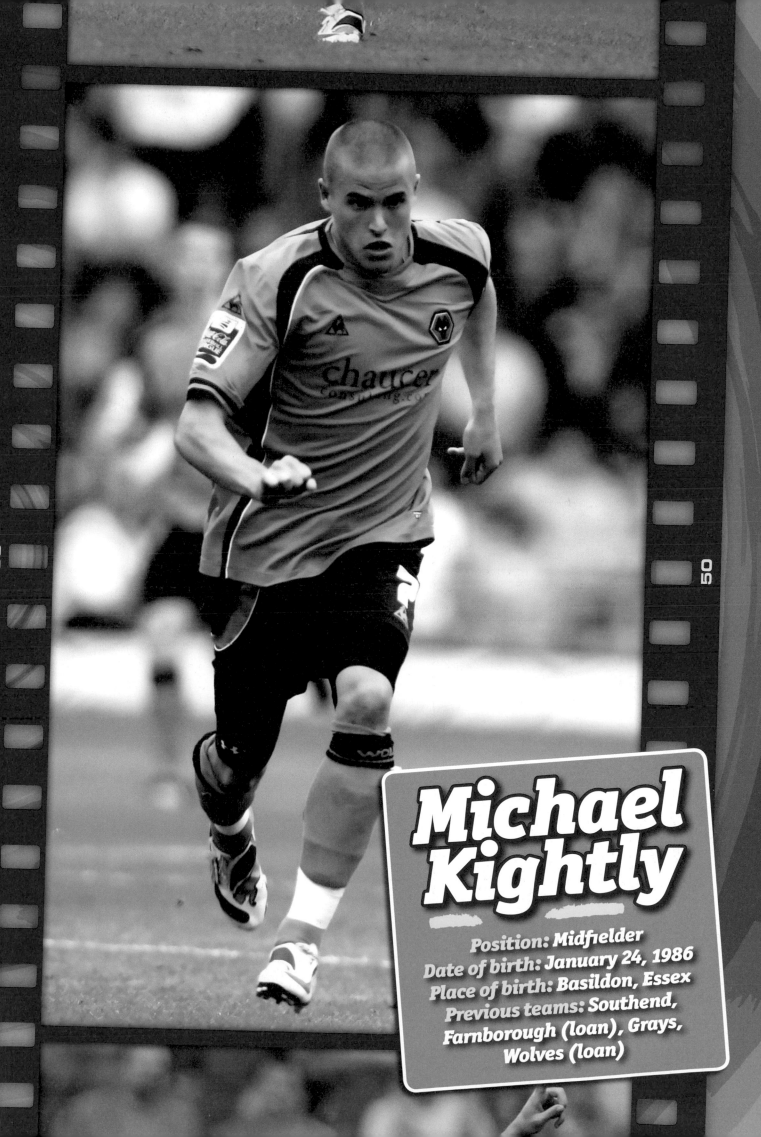

Michael Kightly

Position: Midfielder
Date of birth: January 24, 1986
Place of birth: Basildon, Essex
Previous teams: Southend, Farnborough (loan), Grays, Wolves (loan)

ROARING

WOLVES, ONE OF THE FOOTBALL LEAGUE'S founding members, returned to the Premier League after a five year break after winning the Championship.

AND THEY WILL be hoping their stay in the top-flight is longer than last time! In May 2003 they won the play-off final at Cardiff's Millennium Stadium to earn their place in the Premiership but just a year later they were relegated.

Long-standing chairman Sir Jack Hayward stood down and businessman Steve Morgan - who had failed in a bit to buy Liverpool - bought the Molineux side for just £10... although he had to agree to invest at least £30m in the club!

SPOTLIGHT ON THE CHAMPIONSHIP CHAMPIONS

Wolves gaffer Mick McCarthy says it how he sees it – and it's going to be great hearing what he has to say in the Premier League...

THE GOOD... AFTER THE PROMOTION-CLINCHING WIN AGAINST QPR
"I'm knackered, I'm beaming on the inside, I'm absolutely thrilled by our achievements. I'm very proud of the players, they've been brilliant all season long."

THE BAD... DESPITE A VITAL 3-2 VICTORY AT DERBY COUNTY'S PRIDE PARK!
"We were hopeless. We couldn't have played any worse and yet we won the game. It was bobbins. Quite honestly I thought we were rubbish."

Wolves bites...

- The side in gold clinched the Championship trophy at Barnsley - the town where boss Mick McCarthy was born and the club where he played.

- Kyel Reid, a former Barnsley player, scored the equaliser against the Tykes that gave Wolves the point they needed to take the title.

- Mick McCarthy took Sunderland to Premiership promotion as champions in 2005 but they were relegated the following season.

- Some 50 years ago Wolves legend Billy Wright lifted the old First Division trophy - the same piece of silverware now awarded to Championship winners.

- Winger Michael Kightly missed the final games of the season due to injury but was still named in the PFA's Championship Team of the Season.

WOLVES!

TOP SCORERS

Sylvan Ebanks-Blake (Wolves) 25
Ross McCormack (Cardiff) 21
Jason Scotland (Swansea) 21
Kevin Doyle (Reading) 18

Final Championship table 2008-09

1. Wolves	46	28	90
2. Birmingham	46	17	83
3. Sheff United	46	25	80
4. Reading	46	32	77
5. Burnley	46	12	76
6. Preston	46	12	74
7. Cardiff	46	12	74
8. Swansea	46	13	68
9. Ipswich	46	9	66
10. Bristol City	46	0	61
11. QPR	46	-2	61
12. Sheff Wed	46	-7	61
13. Watford	46	-4	58
14. Doncaster	46	-11	58
15. Crystal Palace	46	-3	57
16. Blackpool	46	-11	56
17. Coventry	46	-11	54
18. Derby	46	-12	54
19. Nottm Forest	46	-15	53
20. Barnsley	46	-13	52
21. Plymouth	46	-13	51
22. Norwich	46	-13	46
23. Southampton	46	-23	45
24. Charlton	46	-22	39

DID YOU KNOW?

All three sides relegated to League One are former Premier League teams! Southampton fell out of the Premier League in 2005 after 27 years in the top-flight. It is their first appearance in the third tier for 50 years.

Charlton, who left the Premiership in May 2007, were last in the third tier in 1981.

Norwich drop to this level for the first time in 49 years, just four years after leaving the top-flight.

SPOTLIGHT ON THE LEAGUE ONE CHAMPIONS

SLY FOXES

MANAGER NIGEL PEARSON was given the boot after just three months in charge at Southampton early in 2008 – despite saving them from relegation during his 14 games in charge.

AND HOW THE Saints must wish that they could now change their minds about that decision!

The former Sheffield Wednesday and Middlesbrough defender – who guided Carlisle to league safety way back in 1999 – took over at Leicester in June 2008 and in his first season won the League One title.

And as the Foxes jumped up a division they saw Southampton drop into League One!

Leicester, who were relegated from the Premier League in 2004, bounced back to the Championship at the first attempt.

TOP SCORERS:

Simon Cox (Swindon Town) 29
Ricky Lambert (Bristol Rovers) 29
Jermaine Beckford
(Leeds United) 27
Matty Fryatt
(Leicester City) 27

Final League One table 2008-09

1	Leicester	46	45	96
2	Peterborough	46	24	89
3	MK Dons	46	36	87
4	Leeds	46	28	84
5	Millwall	46	10	82
6	Scunthorpe	46	19	76
7	Tranmere	46	13	74
8	Southend	46	-3	71
9	Huddersfield	46	-3	68
10	Oldham	46	1	65
11	Bristol Rovers	46	18	63
12	Colchester	46	0	63
13	Walsall	46	-5	61
14	Leyton Orient	46	-12	56
15	Swindon	46	-3	53
16	Brighton	46	-15	52
17	Yeovil	46	-25	51
18	Stockport	46	2	50
19	Hartlepool	46	-13	50
20	Carlisle	46	-13	50
21	Northampton	46	-4	49
22	Crewe	46	-23	46
23	Cheltenham	46	-40	39
24	Hereford	46	-37	34

DID YOU KNOW?

• Peterborough were guided into second spot by manager Darren Ferguson, son of Manchester United's Sir Alex. It was Posh's second successive promotion since he took charge in January 2007.

• Between November 1 and March 11, the Foxes completed a club record unbeaten league run of 23 games. The victory at Southend which clinched promotion was the 13th on their travels, another best.

• MK Dons boss Roberto Di Matteo followed fellow Italians and former Chelsea team-mates Gianluca Vialli and Gianfranco Zola into management.

BUZZING BEES

ANDY SCOTT'S first full season as Griffin Park boss saw Brentford promoted as champions.

THE BEES CLINCHED THE title with a 3-1 victory at Darlington with one game still to play and returned to League One after just two years in the lower division.

Ironically, exactly a year ago Hereford won at Griffin Park to earn promotion themselves – and Bees boss Scott left the dressing room door open so his players could hear the celebrations. He hoped it would inspire his players for the new season! He got that right!

TOP SCORERS:

Grant Holt (Shrewsbury) 20
Jack Lester (Chesterfield) 20
Reuben Reid (Rotherham) 18

Final League Two table 2008-09

1	Brentford	46	29	85
2	Exeter	46	15	79
3	Wycombe	46	21	78
4	Bury	46	20	78
5	Gillingham	46	3	75
6	Rochdale	46	11	70
7	Shrewsbury	46	17	69
8	Dag & Red	46	24	68
9	Bradford	46	11	67
10	Chesterfield	46	5	63
11	Morecambe	46	-3	63
12	Darlington	46	17	62
13	Lincoln City	46	1	59
14	Rotherham	46	14	58
15	Aldershot	46	-21	54
16	Accrington St.	46	-17	50
17	Barnet	46	-18	48
18	Port Vale	46	-22	48
19	Notts County	46	-20	47
20	Macclesfield	46	-32	47
21	Bournemouth	46	8	46
22	Grimsby	46	-18	41
23	Chester	46	-38	37
24	Luton	46	-7	26

DID YOU KNOW?

• Exeter made it two successive promotions under boss Paul Tisdale. It is the fourth time in their 105-year history they have reached the third level.

• Champions Brentford released nine of their title-winning squad when the season ended.

• Wycombe gained automatic promotion on goal difference after tying on points with Bury. Just ONE goal made the difference.

• Wycombe boss Peter Taylor and Exeter director of football Steve Perryman were team-mates at Spurs.

"My right would pop out and pop back in like Mel Gibson's did in Lethal Weapon. I've now probably got the strongest shoulders in the Premier League after all the extra work I have done in the gym. That should help me ride tackles rather than get hit and fall over."

Do you go into tackles harder now?

"In training you obviously don't want to injure your own players so you tend to be a bit softer but matchdays are totally different. If I get clattered that is good for me, even though I know it sounds weird."

STRONG MAN!

ENGLAND FANS will be hoping to see Theo Walcott zooming down the wing, firing in great crosses and weighing in with some spectacular goals. The front man reckons his injury problems are over and that he's now stronger than ever!

Now your shoulder is fixed is that a confidence boost?

"Now it's been fixed, mentally there's nothing wrong in my mind about what might happen. That gives me an extra bit of confidence because I'd known for a while the shoulders could be a problem."

Are you a better player after the injury?

"I'm more of a full grown person and feel stronger than ever. You ask any player in the world and it's the worst feeling being out injured. Fear of failure doesn't bother me. I treat every game the same."

Your future looks good then?

"The boss knows I am learning all of the time. Look at Cristiano Ronaldo. When he came to England people talked about his game being just a few brilliant tricks - now he's the best player in the world."

You looked cool in that penalty shoot-out against Man United?...

"I'm normally at home watching on the telly and want to see games go to penalties for the excitement - but it's not nice, I'm telling you. I had a dry throat going towards the goal but didn't look at the keeper at any time. The best thing to do is just not change your mind."

SPOT THE BALL

WE'VE MADE THE ball disappear from these pictures involving games with top teams. Can you mark which of the squares it was in? Answers page 110

1. MAN CITY v WEST BROM
ROBINHO'S FIRST GOAL OF THE YEAR HELPED CITY TO A 4-2 VICTORY

2. MAN UNITED v EVERTON
RED DEVILS CAME TO A STICKY END IN FA CUP PENALTY SHOOT-OUT AGAINST THE TOFFEES

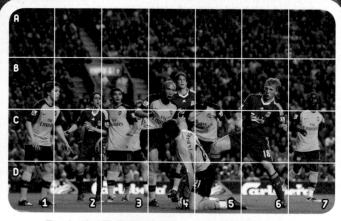

3. LIVERPOOL v ARSENAL
FOUR-MIDABLE ARSHAVIN HIT ALL THE GUNNERS GOALS IN A GLORIOUS 4-4 DRAW

4. BLACKBURN v WIGAN
ROVERS WON LANCASHIRE HOT-POT CLASH 2-0 THANKS TO STRIKES FROM McCARTHY AND NELSEN

5. MAN UNITED v TOTTENHAM
SPURS WENT 2-0 UP BEFORE HALF-TIME BUT LOST 5-2 THRILLER TO FERGIE'S COMEBACK KINGS!

6. WEST HAM v CHELSEA
KALOU'S GOAL WAS THE CLINCHER IN 1-0 VICTORY AT UPTON PARK

7. HULL CITY v LIVERPOOL
**DOUBLE FOR THE DUTCHMAN AS KUYT SCORED
TWICE IN REDS 3-1 MAULING OF THE TIGERS**

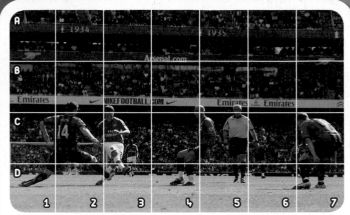

8. ARSENAL v MIDDLESBROUGH
**RED-HOT FABREGAS HIT A BRACE AS GUNNERS
SHOT DOWN BORO 2-0**

9. MAN UNITED v PORTSMOUTH
ROONEY AND CARRICK EASED THE RED DEVILS PAST POMPEY

10. EVERTON v WEST BROM
**SWEET FOR THE TOFFEES THANKS TO
GOALS FROM CAHILL AND SAHA**

11. STOKE CITY v MAN CITY
**TEN-MAN POTTERS TOOK THE SPOILS THANKS
TO BEATTIE'S SIMPLE HEADER**

PAYS TRIBUTE TO THE QUIET MAN OF FOOTBALL

SALUTE SCHOLES!

SCHOLESY STATS

MAN UNITED: 605 appearances, 142 (goals)

ENGLAND: 66 caps (14 goals)

*Correct at end of season 2008-09

FACT: Scholesy isn't always the good guy! He was the first and last England player to be sent off in an international at the old Wembley Stadium.

HONOURS

PREMIER LEAGUE: 1996, 1997, 1999, 2000, 2001, 2003, 2007, 2008, 2009
FA CUP: 1996, 1999, 2004
LEAGUE CUP: 2006, 2009
COMMUNITY SHIELD: 1994, 1996, 1997, 2003, 2008
CHAMPIONS LEAGUE: 1999, 2008
INTERCONTINENTAL CUP: 1999
FIFA CLUB WORLD CUP: 2008

HE'S ONE OF the longest-serving servants of Manchester United yet you have never seen Paul Scholes hit the headlines for anything he has said.

THE QUIET MAN of Old Trafford likes to let his football do the talking and prefers a quiet life rather than go clubbing or be spotted out on the town with his team-mates.

Father-of-three Scholesy would rather spend time with his wife and children – and is one of the most famous followers of Oldham Athletic, where he is often spotted in the stand watching games.

When matches finish he is the first man in the changing room, first out of the showers and first wending his way home. He avoids the media like a plague yet he is one of the most admired midfielders ever to pull on the famous red shirt.

He's one of those rare breed of players who have stayed loyal to a club, having trained with the Red Devils since the age of 14 and then signed a professional contract with them way back in 1993.

TOP TRIBUTES

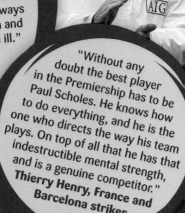

"Many great players have worn the shirt of Manchester United. In so many ways Scholes is my favourite. He's always on the ball. He's always looking to bring other people into the action and if he loses possession you think he must be ill."

Sir Bobby Charlton,
Man United and England legend

"His contribution and his quality and some of the fantastic goals he has scored have been great. He has that wonderful velvet touch on the ball. He has had two knee operations and his eye problem a couple of years ago. He has probably missed more than a year of football."

Sir Alex Ferguson, Man United manager

"Without any doubt the best player in the Premiership has to be Paul Scholes. He knows how to do everything, and he is the one who directs the way his team plays. On top of all that he has that indestructible mental strength, and is a genuine competitor."

Thierry Henry, France and Barcelona striker

KEY DATES

- ⚽ BORN: November 16, 1974, Salford, Manchester
- ⚽ UNITED DEBUT: 21 September 21, 1994, League Cup, at Port Vale
- ⚽ FIRST UNITED GOAL: Two in above 2-1 win
- ⚽ ENGLAND DEBUT: May 24, 1997 v South Africa (friendly), Old Trafford
- ⚽ FIRST ENGLAND GOAL: June 4, 1997, v Italy (friendly)
- ⚽ ENGLAND HAT-TRICK: March 27, 1999 v Poland
- ⚽ ENGLAND RETIREMENT: August 2004
- ⚽ MAJOR TOURNAMENTS: World Cup 1998, 2002; Euro 2000 and 2004.
- ⚽ ENGLISH FOOTBALL HALL OF FAME: September 2008
- ⚽ 600TH MAN UNITED APPEARANCE: April 22, 2009 v Portsmouth

SCHOLESY SAYS...

"I have been lucky to have played with a lot of great players. When you're a young lad, all you want to do is play football with your mates and see your heroes on television playing for England.

It's your wildest dream, so to actually do it, is fantastic. You've got to try and enjoy every minute. Bryan Robson was always my idol, seeing him play for England and scoring goals from midfield. But I was an Oldham fan as a kid and there were people like Andy Ritchie. I used to train every day because at the weekend I would play for three or four teams. I also played for the district, county and school team, and when you look back, you don't know how you turned out every night.

Quiz answers

Puzzle time *page 14*

Get shirty
1. Michael Dawson, Nottingham Forest
2. James Beattie, odd one out
3. Obafemi Martins, Inter Milan
4. Joleon Lescott, Wolves
5. Craig Bellamy, Celtic
6. Jonathan Woodgate, Real Madrid

True or false?
a. True
b. True
c. True
d. False
e. True
f. False
g. True

Crossword *page 26*

Across: 1. Israel 4. France 8. Abou 9. Bobby 10. Gera 13. Kitson 14. Rovers 16. Robinho 18. Andrews 19. Sol 20. Norwich 22. Arbeloa 25. Ekotto 27. Wright 30. Eto'o 31. Train. 32. Bent 33. Barmby 34. Arsene.

Down: 2. Scott 3. Lion 4. Fabio 5. Cresswell 6. Parker 7. Davies 11. John 12. Reid 15. Posh 17. Barcelona 18. Alan 20. Nelsen 21. Iron 23. Bury 24. Arteta 26. Terry 28. Green 29. FIFA.

Spot the Ball *page 32*
1. A4, 2. D7, 3. D4, 4. A4, 5. A4, 6. B3, 7. A4, 8. A7, 9. A14, 10. D4, 11. C5

Know your football *page 38*

Who am I?
1. Nani
2. Robinho
3. Kaka
4. Jo
5. Denilson
6. Deco

Match the team
A. West Ham United
B. Blackburn Rovers
C. Plymouth Argyle
D. Brighton and Hove Albion
E. West Bromwich Albion
F. Ipswich Town

No place like home

Nottingham Forest
• Picture C, City Ground
Blackburn Rovers
• Picture D, Ewood Park
Newcastle United
• Picture F, St. James' Park
Derby County
• Picture E, Pride Park
Wolves
• Picture A, Molineux
West Ham
• Picture B, Upton Park

A-Z Quiz *page 48*
A. Arsenal
B. South Africa
C. Carlo Cudicini
D. Derby County
E. Eduardo
F. Fulham
G. Everton
H. Hartlepool
I. Zlatan Ibrahimovich
J. Jermaine Jenas
K. Kaka
L. Liverpool
M. Jose Mourinho
N. Nigel Clough (son of Brian)
O. Leyton Orient
P. Pompey (Portsmouth)
Q. QPR
R. Robbie (Keane)
S. Stadium of Light (Sunderland)
T. Turkey
U. Underhill
V. Villans (Aston Villa)
W. Wembley
X. Xisco
Y. Luke Young
Z. Gianfranco Zola

Blasts from the past! *page 54*
A. Freddie Ljungberg
B. Mark Hughes
C. Michael Owen
D. Alan Shearer
E. David Beckham
F. Roy Keane
G. Steve Bruce
H. Sam Allardyce
I. Gordon Strachan
J. Gary Megson

Spot the Ball *page 106*
1. A3, 2. A4, 3. A6, 4. A2, 5. D4, 6.D3, 7. C1, 8. C4, 9. C10, 10. A2, 11. B5